PRESSURE POINTS

Other books by J. D. Payne

Missional House Churches

The Barnabas Factors

Discovering Church Planting

Evangelism

Roland Allen

Kingdom Expressions

Strangers Next Door

PRESSURE POINTS

Twelve Global Issues Shaping
the Face of the Church

J. D. Payne

Published in Nashville, Tennessee, by Thomas Nelson. Thomas Nelson is a registered trademark of Thomas Nelson, Inc.

Typesetting by Rainbow Graphics, Kingsport, Tennessee.

Thomas Nelson, Inc., titles may be purchased in bulk for educational, business, fund-raising, or sales promotional use. For information, please e-mail SpecialMarkets@ThomasNelson.com.

Unless otherwise noted, Scripture quotations are taken from THE ENGLISH STANDARD VERSION. © 2001 by Crossway Bibles, a division of Good News Publishers.

Scripture quotations marked KJV are from the King James Version.

ISBN: 978-1-4185-5074-5

Printed in the United States of America

13 14 15 16 17 18 RRD 6 5 4 3 2 1

To my heavenly Father,
and to my earthly partner, Sarah

Contents

Foreword

There are 7,072,622,454 and counting.

As I write this foreword, this is the population of the world. According to the most liberal estimates, approximately one-third of the world is Christian. These estimates include all who identify themselves as Christian, whether religiously, socially, or politically. Likely, not all of them are actually followers of Christ. Even if we assume they are, that still leaves 4.7 billion people who (if the gospel is true) are at this moment separated from God in their sins and who (assuming nothing changes) will spend eternity in hell.

Again, 4.7 billion.

Meanwhile, Christ has commissioned His church to make disciples among all of them—literally, in every nation and amid every people. God has created, saved, and called each of His children to proclaim His gospel to all of the world. And He has guaranteed the success of their mission. All of history is heading toward the day when ransomed men and women from every nation, tribe, people, and language will bow down around the throne of God to give Him the praise that He alone is due for the salvation that He alone can give.

Consequently, it is incumbent upon every Christian and every church to be aware of the issues, opportunities, challenges, and obstacles that we face in the eventual accomplishment of this Great Commission. If we are going to obediently and meaningfully impact the world around us with the gospel that has been entrusted to us, then we must be cognizant of *what* God is sovereignly doing around the world and *how* God is graciously calling us to join with Him in His work.

For this reason, I am deeply thankful for this book. I don't know another person who pays more attention to global trends and spends more time considering how they affect the local church than J. D. Payne. He is a scholar and a friend, a fellow pastor and a trusted co-laborer. The issues he addresses in this book are massive in scope, yet he frames each of them with confidence in the majesty of the merciful God who knows all things, ordains all things, and will eventually use all things to achieve His ultimate purpose.

I hope and pray that *Pressure Points* will be a wake-up call to our lives and churches alerting us to what God is doing in the world and calling us to engage that world more effectively with the gospel of God's great grace for the glory of God's great name.

David Platt

Introduction

The Church and the Pressures of the Age

Recently, my family and I moved to Birmingham, Alabama, where I have the honor to serve as one of the pastors of The Church at Brook Hills. Prior to our move, my wife, Sarah, and I traveled to the city in search of a house. After the crazy house-hunting exercise, we finally decided on an older one surrounded by a wooded lot. I had always heard about the damage that tree roots could do to concrete, but I had not thought much about it until walking around this property. One tree in our front yard has part of its root system running under our driveway. Over time the roots of this tree started applying pressure to the ground under the driveway and thus to the driveway itself. Finally, at a time long before we purchased the house, the force was so strong that the roots broke our driveway in half lifting the separated piece of concrete about five inches above the ground.

Pressure is a unique and powerful force. Without an appropriate blood pressure, the human body cannot function. Every jeweler knows that when carbon is placed under the appropriate amount of heat and pressure, a diamond can result. Water pressure has been called one of the deadliest forces in the universe, but without it we would not have running water in our homes and buildings.

I decided to use the metaphor of pressure in the title of this book because pressure can be both damaging and beneficial. The question for the church to consider today is, how should she live in such an age with a multitude of matters applying pressure?

What I have done in this work is identify what I believe to be twelve of the most critical matters facing the church in the first half of the twenty-first century, each greatly influencing the advancement of the gospel across the nations of the world. While my list is not exhaustive, neither are these mutually exclusive. For example, globalization and the growth of cities are closely connected. The growth of cities, poverty, and the pornification of societies influence one another. While I separate these for the sake of this book's organization, many are tightly connected.

Until the Lord's return, each generation of believers will face numerous challenges to the mission of the church. While the church does not have control over the macro-level contextual issues of each generation, her response to them is a matter of kingdom stewardship. She can either allow the pressure from these global issues to push her off of her biblical moorings and into a place of irrelevancy, or, like a flywheel that continues to pick up momentum as pressure is applied to it, she can discern the pressures and prayerfully consider a response while remaining faithful to her Lord. While each of today's critical issues poses numerous challenges to the advancement of the gospel, I write this work with a positive tone, believing that some of the greatest days for kingdom advancement are still to come.

Challenges of the Age

Ever since the first century, the church has experienced challenges to her mission of making disciples of all nations. Shortly after Pentecost, persecution arose against the believers (Acts 4:1–3). Later, internal struggles along racial lines developed (Acts 6:1). Peter would have to be convinced by a vision and voice from God that He was concerned about the Gentiles (Acts 10). Such tension between the Jewish and Gentile churches called the Jerusalem Council to provide guidance as to how the matter should be resolved (Acts 15:1–35) and fellowship maintained.

Sexual immorality plagued the first-century churches (1 Cor. 5:1; Rev. 2:20). Some churches struggled with material wealth and apathy (Rev. 3:15–19). Others struggled with false teachings (Gal. 1:6–7; 2 John 7–11). Neither were the churches immune to the external problems of famine (Acts 11:27–30) and poverty (Acts 3:2; Gal. 2:10).

The pressures of the sinfulness of man, the opposition of the devil, the groanings of a broken world, and the twisted ungodly world system may at times slow the growth of the church, but they will never crush the bride of Christ. In the economy of the King, the pressure of such opposition often brings about manifestations of His grace revealing His magnificent omnipotence.

Over the past two thousand years, the church has constantly found herself swimming in a sea of difficulties and delights, challenges and comforts, opposition and opportunities. The call to become a follower of Jesus is a call to membership in the church. And the journey from the moment of one's conversion to glorification is a life lived on mission as a world-impacting disciple maker. While Jesus promised that with the coming of the Spirit, we would be able to do even greater things than Himself (John 14:12), He also reminded us that as long as we are in the world there will be challenges and pressures applying much force to us—His church. Yet we are to take heart for He has overcome the world (John 16:33) and is able to present us blameless before God (Jude 24). We are not alone. In every age, in every location, the church has experienced pressures affecting the mission of making disciples of all nations. And even when the expansion of the kingdom seemed nonexistent, Jesus' promise that He would build His church remains (Matt. 16:18).

The Stewardship of Innovation

For better or for worse, the global issues of our day are shaping and will continue to shape the church. In light of the growth of the cities, how will the church make disciples of the nations there? What unique Great Commission opportunities now exist that 214 million people have migrated outside of their countries of birth? What does the church need to be doing now in sub-Saharan Africa in light of the large number of children with HIV? How does the growth of Islam influence the way the church is to be on mission today? How do we teach new believers the way of Jesus in light of the pornification of their context? These are just a few of the multitude of questions that we should be asking—with more to come—in view of the global issues around us today.

This book is written not only to raise awareness, but to challenge the church to ask questions and to submit humbly to the Lord, crying out for wisdom, discernment, and guidance in view of the pressures that surround us. In our integrated world, the global issues are not ones that we can say are "over there" and not in our own communities. Such issues do not limit themselves to geographical borders. And with each pressure comes an invitation to make necessary changes in how we make disciples of all nations. With each of our global issues, the church is faced with a decision: follow the leadership of the Spirit and innovate methodologically and strategically or remain on the present course. The choice to follow the latter option is usually a recipe for the hindrance of gospel advancement and church multiplication across North America and throughout the world. The call to follow Jesus is a call to remove from our vocabularies the phrase "We've never done it that way before." He is a dynamic Savior with His Spirit at work in and through the pressure points of our age. Innovations—even in missions—often take people in new directions while building on the labors of those who have gone before. Across the ages, the church has been innovating for gospel advancement in light of the pressure points of the day. Some examples of this include working deep in the heart of countries and not simply along the coastlines, using literature, radio, audio recordings, satellites, medicine, agricultural science, crusades, storying, business as mission, and the development of the discipline of missiology. But before we come to believe that the church is to innovate using the methods of the world or to innovate simply for innovation's sake to stay cool and hip, we must remember that such is not the case.

In the book of Acts, we read that innovation was a matter of following the leadership of the Spirit of mission. For example, Peter had to make internal and external adjustments when it came to spending time with the God-fearing Gentiles (Acts 10). The birth of the church in Antioch (Acts 11) resulted in overcoming persecution and crossing the racial divide into the world of the Gentiles. The church in Philippi was birthed after the team made two attempts to preach elsewhere and eventually engaged some women at a place of prayer, rather than a crowd in a synagogue (Acts 16). Throughout the Scriptures—and across history—believers are often required to change their general ways of thinking and functioning for the health of the church and gospel advancement. Structures, institutions, organizations, and traditions are to remain nimble and held loosely. It is when the church resists Spirit-led change and the need to innovate in light of global circumstances that she soon finds herself impotent and in poor health.

Unfortunately, such adjustments are usually painful and difficult. Christians are the ultimate conservatives when it comes to making necessary institutional adjustments for missions. And—it is sad to write—in many cases, until our pet preferences become a burden to us, or are cataclysmically removed from our control, we are likely to hold on to them, grieving the Spirit yet believing we are walking the straight-and-narrow path for gospel advancement. We are often guilty of taking what the Spirit provides for kingdom advancement and, over time, turning it into an idol for which we will sacrifice our lives.

The body must always be growing in conformity to the Head, and innovation is required with such growth. We innovate for the advancement of the gospel as the pressures of the age apply force and create challenges to the mission of the church. Just as the history of humanity is filled with examples of innovation that resulted in breakthroughs that reshaped society, the church's innovations in missions will continue to result in breakthroughs that will glorify the Lord and reshape the bride as she waits for the Groom.

Adjustments for a Changing World

We live in a time of unprecedented political, educational, technological, economical, and medical change. Consider any discipline, and you are likely to find that great developments have occurred in that field over the past twenty years. What used to seem a big, big world is now a small world after all. As stewards of the mysteries of God, our trustworthiness not only involves our faithfulness with the great truths we have received, but also how we will wisely share this whole counsel of God in a world of pressures. With four billion people in the world who are not kingdom citizens—including over two billion who have never heard the name *Jesus*—we have much to do in our day. Knowing how to live as wise stewards involves knowing our world in light of our commission. Knowing our world means understanding the global pressure points shaping the face of the church and mission.

1

Unreached People Groups

The Bread of Life is simply not available to
hundreds and hundreds of millions of people.

—David A. Fraser[1]

One summer I flew into Montreal and then made a ten-hour drive into the Gaspé region of Quebec. Quebec is a province just across the US-Canadian border with a population of about seven million Quebecois—an unreached people comprised of an estimated 0.8 percent evangelical population. For the next week a team and I worked with one of the few believing families in the peninsula in the areas of outreach, evangelism, and looking for "people of peace" (Luke 10:5–7) with whom to begin a Bible study that would hopefully become a church.

On another trip I found myself navigating the public transportation system of London with its high numbers of people. I rode the tube and walked the sidewalks in one of the largest cities in Western Europe. Within the shadow of Big Ben is Fatimah, a resident of West London, a student, a Muslim who makes an annual pilgrimage to Mecca, and a representative of an unreached people group.

While walking the streets of Paris, members of our evangelism team ventured into another part of the city from our location. While there they encountered many Turks and were able to enter into several conversations about the gospel, with a couple coming to faith in Jesus that day. The Turks have been described as the largest unreached people group in the world. Karem Kroc, pastor of the Antalya Protestant Church in Antalya, Turkey, believes that there are only about twenty-five hundred believers among the seventy-five million Muslims in Turkey alone.[2]

The concept of people groups (including unreached people groups) is as old as the Old Testament that describes the unbelieving nations living around Israel. Even though popular discussions of unreached people groups can be traced back to 1974, there are still four billion people on the earth who do not have a relationship with Jesus, including over two billion who have never even heard the name *Jesus*. While the gospel has been advancing among the unreached peoples of the world, the high number of remote populations remains a pressure point for the church today.

Nations: from *Countries* to *Peoples*

For many years the church interpreted *nations* in Jesus' Great Commission (Matt. 28:18–20) as meaning literal nation-states or countries. For example, Israel would be considered a nation. Egypt would be another. Libya another. To "go therefore and make disciples of all nations" was understood to be the going into a geopolitical area of the world, and as long as some people became followers of Jesus in that country, then that nation had been reached with the gospel.

However, in the mid-twentieth century, many began to question this interpretation and started advocating that the Greek expression *ta ethne* was to be understood not as countries on a map with their national boundaries (which are known to change) but as ethnic groups.

Taken in this light, Jesus' commission to make disciples of all the nations was not fulfilled when all of the countries of the world had some believers living within their boundaries. Now the church began to realize that a country such as Russia was not simply made up of Russians but consisted of Abaza, Digor, Kazakh, and Tajik, just to mention a few of the 170 peoples living there. India was not comprised of South Asian Indians but a multitude of various ethnic groups representing many languages, castes, and tribes. When such understandings of the biblical text began to be embraced, suddenly the *ta ethne* of Matthew 28:19 did not refer to the independent countries recognized by the United Nations in the 1950s but to thousands of ethnic groups speaking thousands of different languages and dialects.

While missiologist Ralph Winter was not the first to acknowledge this interpretation of the biblical text or the number of such groups in the world, his presentation at the 1974 Lausanne Congress on World Evangelization inspired and moved a multitude of evangelicals from across the globe to rethink what is necessary to make disciples of all nations.

Winter, in his presentation titled, "The Highest Priority: Cross-Cultural Evangelism," emphasized that there were thousands of *hidden peoples* in the world and, apart from cross-cultural missionary activity, they would never have a chance to hear and respond to the gospel. Seven years after his movement-making address in Lausanne, Switzerland, Winter wrote, "These peoples are being called the 'Hidden Peoples' and are defined by ethnic or sociological traits to be people so different from the cultural traditions of any existing church that missions (rather than evangelism) strategies are necessary for the planting of indigenous churches within their particular traditions."[3]

By the 1980s, numerous evangelicals were advocating the importance of understanding and reaching the hidden peoples. Individuals such as Ed Dayton, C. Peter Wagner, and Luis Bush were just a few of the several outspoken leaders advocating this new direction in missions. Many mission agencies began to rethink their evangelization strategies and reoriented themselves to getting the gospel to the "10/40 Window," an imaginary perimeter on the globe where the majority of the world's hidden peoples live. Over time the nomenclature shifted, and hidden peoples became known as *unreached peoples* or *unreached people groups* (UPGs).

What Is a *People Group*?

While the words *people group* have been in use for many years now, it is still helpful to begin with a definition and description. Just because words are frequently used does not mean that most hearers (and users) know the meaning of those words. The Lausanne Committee for World Evangelization defines a people group as "the largest group through which the gospel can flow without encountering significant barriers of acceptance or understanding." The LCWE goes on to explain that such groups may be defined in a variety of ways including language, culture, history, geography, and position in society. India with her caste system is a good example of this final category; the caste system transcends language, ethnicity, and geography.[4]

Unengaged and Unreached

For the most part, missiologists hold to one of two related definitions of what constitutes an *unreached people*. The first definition would label a group unreached if less than 2 percent of that people group were evangelical and less than 5 percent of that people group considered themselves adherents to Christianity. For example, according to Joshua Project, of the thirty-seven million French in France, only 0.9 percent are evangelical, but 67 percent claim an adherence to Christianity. Because of the adherence rate, Joshua Project considers this group to be reached.

The second commonly used definition of an unreached people group, and the one to which I hold, states that a people is unreached if they are less than 2 percent evangelical, with the adherence rate not a consideration. According to this definition, the French people with an evangelical percentage of 0.9 percent would most definitely be considered unreached.

Christians are on every continent and in every country in the world. With such a multitude of believers, it would seem that there would be few unreached people groups in the world. Such is not the case, even with the amazing growth of the church in the Majority World (see chapter 3). Members of the Lausanne Committee for World Evangelization helped explain this present pressure point:

> Despite the appearance that Christianity is everywhere, the truth is that at least one-quarter of humanity still has little or no access to the good news of Jesus Christ. These least reached are members of over 6,000 (out of about 16,000) distinct people groups whose languages, cultures and/or location have isolated them from believers in significantly more reached people groups living in their own countries and in others around the world. . . .
>
> These people groups, however, have virtually no choice with respect to the gospel. They fail to follow the One who said "Follow Me," not because they have rejected that call, but because they have never heard it. While many UPGs are relatively small in size (approximately 1/2 have populations of less than 10,000 each), at least 1,000 of these least reached people groups have populations of more than 100,000 each. More than 250 of them have populations exceeding one million each![5]

The term *unengaged* is a helpful addition to our nomenclature, for it assists in focusing our vision on the task at hand. Of the six thousand–plus unreached people groups in the world, some of them, while still less than 2 percent evangelical, have missionaries and churches among them. The word *unengaged* (often expressed as *unengaged-unreached*) brings our attention to those peoples with whom no one is applying any intentional evangelical church multiplication strategy. While prayer and advocacy for such groups are important, these two matters alone do not remove a group from the unengaged category.

There are three main databases from which we obtain our information on the unreached peoples of the world. The World Christian Database,[6] Joshua Project,[7] and Global Research Department of the International Mission Board[8] have similar collections that are constantly being updated in light of new global realities. At the time of this writing, Global Research tells us there are

- 11,342 total people groups;
- 6,422 unreached people groups (not including the United States and Canada);
- 571 unreached people groups in the United States and Canada; and
- 3,133 unreached-unengaged people groups.[9]

Why Evangelicals?

I am periodically asked why missiologists count evangelical Christians specifically whenever they evaluate reached and unreached people groups. The reason is simply that it is the easiest benchmark when attempting to measure a global population of billions of people. There are people who have repented of sin and placed their faith in Jesus and are part of Christian traditions who would not describe themselves as evangelical. And, to be fair, there are people who claim to be evangelical who have not been born again. No one claims that the evangelical benchmark is without its limitations. However, since understanding the global status of world evangelization is based on knowing who has been regenerated by the Holy Spirit and is likely to carry the gospel to others, the easiest way to determine this group is by identifying who is an evangelical.[10]

Where Is Our Priority?

The Church at Brook Hills recently completed a study of the book of Revelation. This book challenges us to think about how we should live now as we look forward to the second coming of the Lord. One matter that we all must keep in mind is that as we await His return, there are multitudes who do not yet know about His first coming. We live in a world where over two billion people have never heard the gospel. Even with the hundreds of thousands of missionaries serving in the world today and decades of discussions related to unreached people groups, it is estimated that only 10 percent of the evangelical missionary force is doing pioneer mission work among unreached people groups. That means that nine times as many missionaries are serving among the reached people groups as among the unreached.[11] To help put things in a different perspective, only about 14 percent of Buddhists, 14 percent of Hindus, 13 percent of Muslims, and 19 percent of all of those who are non-Christian know a Christian.[12] It has also been estimated that 82 percent of Christian monies collected goes to home pastoral ministries, mainly in Europe and the Americas. Twelve percent goes to domestic missions. Less than 6 percent is spent on missions outside of these heavily Christianized regions. But only 0.1 percent goes toward the unevangelized world![13]

Our treasures are located where our passions, desires, energies, and very selves are found (Matt. 6:21). In view of the urgency of the gospel and the lostness of the peoples, clearly our priorities are not in the proper order. Can we say that we are Great Commission Christians whenever we manifest such poor stewardship? Such numbers reveal a most unwise use of our resources of people, money, and time in light of Jesus' mandate to us and the pressure point of seven thousand unreached people groups.

Strangers Next Door

Each year Western nations receive peoples from all over the world, many of whom represent some of the world's unreached people groups. When I wrote *Strangers Next Door: Immigration, Migration, and Mission,* I wanted to raise awareness of the numbers of the unreached peoples who have been immigrating to the West. Including the 571 unreached people groups in the United States and Canada, I estimate that representatives from 1,200 unreached people groups are presently living in North America, Western Europe, Australia, and New Zealand. This is a wonderful opportunity for the church to serve the nations. The opportunities for reaching out to those with the love of Christ are numerous and come with little challenges and opposition. While the greatest need for gospel advancement and church planting remains outside of the West, we must not forget that many of the unreached peoples have moved next door. Unfortunately for many churches, these peoples remain strangers to them.

While the pressure point of international migration is discussed in chapter 5, it is important in this chapter to draw attention to the reality of migration of unreached people groups. The nations have been migrating to unassuming locations. For example, Louisville, Kentucky, is home to many representatives of unreached people groups. When I lived there, our church regularly encountered Palestinians, Bosnians, Somalis, Nepalese,

South Asian Indians, Japanese, and Chinese, to name a few. Just as the Lord has told us to go into all of the world and make disciples of the peoples, He has also brought many unreached peoples to our neighborhoods.

While writing this section of the book, I received a request from someone asking for guidance for his church regarding reaching South Asians living in his city in Ohio. He noted that many Bhutanese had been baptized and a church planted with them. Also, he and other believers were reaching out to many Indians living in the area and had observed four young Hindus make professions of faith in Jesus.

May such stories among the unreached peoples increase as churches make disciples of all nations, whether across the street or across the world! Whether laboring in their own neighborhood or in other nations, cross-cultural labors are an absolute necessity for churches.

Cross-Cultural Disciple Making Needed

For decades missiologists have classified disciple-making work according to the cultural distance between the one doing the work of an evangelist and those hearing the gospel. Each week that our church gathers for worship, an invitation is extended to those present to repent and place faith in Jesus. This is usually given during the sermon or at its conclusion. This type of evangelism is referred to as E-0, since generally speaking the culture is very similar for those present at our worship gathering. However, when I share the gospel with a white, middle-class American doing some construction work on my house, this category is E-1. It is evangelism done among those of my culture but outside of a local church gathering. The team that I helped lead to the Gaspé region of Quebec to work among the Quebecois was engaged in cross-cultural work, for they were not like us, culturally speaking. But as we were all

North Americans and European descendants, our cultural differences were not significant. Similarly, those of us on the team in Paris working among the national Parisians found ourselves in a similar-yet-different context. Clearly there were cultural differences, but they were not stark differences. This type of evangelism has been categorized as E-2. Whenever our church sends a team to work among the Somalis in Minneapolis or the Han in China, we encounter cultural gaps are so wide that disciple making at this level is known as E-3.

The most needed type of disciple making today is found in the E-2 and E-3 categories both within North America and in other countries. Until the churches scattered across the world are willing to reach out and cross both slightly different and significantly different cultural barriers to share the love of Jesus, the unreached will remain unreached. Whether it is the Chinese church in San Francisco reaching across the bay area into the Afghani community, the African American church in downtown Chicago taking the gospel to the Guatemalans in their neighborhood, or the Korean church in rural Georgia preaching the truth among the Fulakunda in Senegal, cross-cultural work is the need of the hour.

Whether the church is in the United States or the Ukraine, this pressure point is a reminder to us that the church must become more and more cross-cultural in her global disciple-making efforts. Churches in Indonesia are going to have to bridge cultural gaps in order to reach into the Muslim people groups living on Java. Parisian believers must move from their comfort zones into the world of the Algerians living down the street from them or in North Africa. The unengaged-unreached have no known churches working among them; those that will work among them will have to do E-2 and E-3 labors.

As churches pray for the unreached peoples and for the Lord's guidance in reaching them, they also need to be intentional in their outreach efforts. Without intention to act, rarely does action occur. It is also important that we learn as we go. Cross-cultural work, whether in the United States or Iran, is filled with inevitable mistakes. We should be prepared to make mistakes and remain humble as we go into all the world. Part of learning is understanding the cultural differences and striving to contextualize our methods from people to people. The pressure point of the unengaged and unreached in our world today will continue to shape the church in the way she does missions and her future membership. Of course this should not surprise us, for we have already been told of the multiethnic congregation in heaven (Rev. 7:9). And while "every nation" is represented at the great wedding feast, there are nations that have yet to receive the wedding invitation. What a wonderful opportunity to be a part of seeing John's great vision come to pass as we invite them to the table!

Questions to Consider

1. What are you and your church doing to engage the unengaged and reach the unreached peoples of the world?

2. Was it a surprise to you that so many unreached people groups are now living in Western nations? If they are reached with the gospel, what is the potential for kingdom advancement if they carry this hope to their loved ones back in their countries of birth?

3. Are you looking around your neighborhood for possible unreached people groups? If not, why not? If so, who is living there and how will you begin to lead your church to reach out to them?

4. Are you and your church ready to engage in E-2 and E-3 labors across the street and across the world? If you are already involved in such efforts, what are you learning from your labors that have worked well and those that have not worked so well? What do you need to share

with others based on your experiences? What do you need to learn from others? What will you do today to start this learning process?

5. How do you feel knowing that your church could be directly responsible for seeing certain nations—foreseen by John in Revelation—in heaven?

CHAPTER 2

The West
as a Mission Field

The West is, once again, a vast mission field.

—GEORGE G. HUNTER III[1]

For nearly two hundred years, the great Protestant missionary movement swept from the West to the East, or what is now referred to as the Majority World. Now, however, the post-Christian West[2] has become a major mission field. Within recent decades, the church in the Western nations of the world has been experiencing a significant decline in both adherents to the faith and influence on society at large. While such declines have been the most drastic outside the United States, the impact is clearly felt in this country.

From Carey . . .

The Modern Protestant Missionary Movement began in 1792 with the publication of William Carey's *An Enquiry into the Obligation of Christians to Use Means for the Conversion of the Heathens.* The following year, Carey, John Thomas, and their families set sail for India. While this was not the first effort of Protestants to go into all the world to make disciples, it was a turning point in the history of Christian missions. Now the English-speaking world was entering the foreign missionary

13

enterprise and developing mission societies from which they would work.

For the following centuries the Protestant missionary force would primarily come from the Western world, particularly England and the United States, with the latter remaining the largest missionary-sending country in the world well into the twenty-first century. The years following Carey's publication saw a massive surge of missionaries making great sacrifices for the advancement of the gospel. What started as a handful of believers has grown to a force of several hundred thousand career missionaries serving in some of the most difficult locations on the planet and representing thousands of churches and mission agencies.

While such fervor was taking place, the West was also facing the rise of ideologies that would contribute to the dwindling influence of the church in society. Secularism, modernity, and later postmodern thought and practice facilitated the demise of Christendom. Pluralism became commonplace, and Lesslie Newbigin (missionary, author, and general secretary of the International Missionary Council) reflected on this reality:

> The gospel is news of what has happened. The problem of communicating it in a pluralist society is that it simply disappears into the undifferentiated ocean of information. It represents one opinion among millions of others. It cannot be 'the truth,' since in a pluralist society truth is not one but many. It may be 'true for you,' but it cannot be true for everyone. To claim that it is true for everyone is simply arrogance. It is permitted as one opinion among many.[3]

As time progressed, the shadow of the steeple shrank across the West and the chime of church bells grew faint. France, Germany, England, Scotland, Denmark, and Switzerland—places once considered bastions of theological orthodoxy and zealous missionary advancement—were now spiritual deserts with only a small percent of evangelicals. While the United States is not the great white savior, evangelicals here remain the largest in number and vibrancy in the Western world. However, Barna released a report noting that many Americans are very concerned about restrictions in religious freedoms. Twenty-nine percent of all US adults and 71 percent of evangelicals are also very concerned about religious freedoms being more restricted in the next five years in this country.[4] This is not a Christian country but a nation of a multitude of peoples from many nations with many desperately in need of gospel transformation.

. . . to Newbigin

The story of Lesslie Newbigin is one of a man living on the edge of the transition of the West from a place of missionary sending to missionary receiving. After serving almost forty years as a missionary to India (1936–1974), Newbigin returned home to a different England. Like the theoretical astronaut who travels from earth at the speed of light and returns a few minutes later only to find that everyone has aged significantly, Newbigin arrived home to find a people with a different and quickly changing worldview. The influence and value of the church on society had been diminished significantly. Matters of faith had been relegated to the sphere of private life—and were to be kept there.

Newbigin was witnessing changes in the minds and hearts of many across the Western world. Modernity was giving way to postmodernity with its understanding of a truth that is constructed by societies and is thus relativistic and not universal. Life in the West was seen as more refined, and "superstitious ways" such as faith practices were not needed. Newbigin felt so strongly about the changes in the West that he wrote, "It would seem, therefore, that there is no higher priority for the research work of missiologists than to ask the question of what would be involved in a genuinely missionary encounter between the gospel and this modern Western culture."[5]

Newbigin was not the first to call attention to the post-Christian West, but would become very influential in challenging the church in the West to rethink how she should respond to her mission now that the Western world had become post-churched or post-Christian. Newbigin's solution to the present realities was that the church needed to think of the West as a context in need of missionary activity and not a reached environment.

Post-Christian Mission Field

Since Newbigin's experience, at least two generations in the United States have grown up under the ideology of postmodernity: Generation X and the Millennials. Their worldviews and lifestyles are quite unlike their parents' and grandparents'—the Baby Boomers and the Builders, respectively. Beginning with the Builder generation born before 1945, the United States has witnessed a declining rate of conversion among each subsequent generation. Now a massive one-third of adults under thirty years of age subscribe to no religious affiliation.[6]

We find ourselves well entrenched in a society that dichotomizes faith into the public and private spheres. I remember sitting in a coffee shop in Newfoundland with a couple who were not followers of Jesus. After we had been discussing the gospel for some time, the man, Shaun, responded, "That is great! I am so delighted that you have found something like that for your life. It is just not for me. What I believe is fine." I have often heard variations on this theme: "What's good for you is good—as long as you keep it to yourself—and what's good for me is good as well." Yes, it is okay to pray at an inauguration or during a day of mourning, but for the most part the West now desires to keep faith matters relegated to the private life of individuals. It is fine if you want to go and worship on Sunday, but make sure you do not bring your faith matters to work on Monday.

The West advocates that truth is socially constructed and may only exist for a season, rather than a universal factor applicable to all peoples at all times. The religious books of any faith tradition claiming to hold such universal truths (metanarrative) are considered to have little relevance for today. Morality is a matter of personal preference as long as no one gets hurt. And personal pleasure, rather than objective matters of right and wrong, is king. Denial of self-gratification is understood as negative, for we now live in societies that are self-therapeutic, advocating hedonistic lifestyles—at least in private.

In the Western world the United States has the highest concentration of evangelicals. According to the Pew Forum on Religion and Public Life, evangelicals make up 26 percent of this country.[7] In Canada the number is about 8 percent, Australia is 14 percent, and New Zealand is18 percent. Evangelicals comprise very low numbers in Western European countries. For example, the United Kingdom is 9 percent evangelical; Denmark, 4 percent; Netherlands, 4 percent; Switzerland, 4 percent; Germany, 2 percent; Spain, 1 percent; and France, 1 percent.[8]

Of course these are nationwide percentages. The compositions change from location to location. For example, while the Prairie Provinces of Canada have higher concentrations of evangelicals, Quebec has a provincial percentage of 0.8 percent, making it by far the least evangelical province of the country. Though the United States' average is 26 percent, states such as Alabama, Oklahoma, and Mississippi have much higher percentages of around 40 percent. Utah, Rhode Island, and Massachusetts are between 2 and 3 percent.

Least Evangelical US States, 2010[9]

State	Evangelical Percentage
Utah	2.3
Rhode Island	2.5
Massachusetts	3.4
New Hampshire	3.6
Vermont	3.6
New Jersey	4.3
Connecticut	4.4
Maine	4.5
New York	4.5
Delaware	7.2

From 35,000 to 15,000 Feet

Whenever you fly over a small town at thirty-five thousand feet, you get a radically different perspective than when walking the streets of that town. At such an altitude you are able to see the border of the town. You are able to distinguish the industrial park, the downtown core, suburban subdivisions, and baseball and football fields. However, you are unable to locate the local grocery store, McDonald's, or sporting goods shop. To discern such details, you must lower the altitude and land the plane.

Nationwide numbers showing religious adherents provide us with the thirty-five-thousand-feet perspective. If we lower the plane and then observe the numbers at that height, we quickly realize that the 26 percent evangelical count in the United States is not common across the country. Though statewide levels do provide us a more detailed picture, consider the following table that shows the least-reached urban contexts in the United States.

Urban Contexts in the United States under 5 Percent Evangelical[10]

METRO AREA	Evangelical Totals	Percent of Evangelicals
Provo-Orem, UT	2,540	0.5
Logan, UT-ID	1,746	1
St. George, UT	2,345	2
Pittsfield, MA	2,817	2
Kingston, NY	4,104	2
Barnstable Town, MA	5,281	3
Salt Lake City, UT	29,498	3
Providence-New Bedford-Fall River, RI-MA	45,007	3
Boston-Cambridge-Quincy, MA-NH	146,838	3
Norwich-New London, CT	9,320	3
Ogden-Clearfield, UT	18,689	3
Glens Falls, NY	4,502	4
Utica-Rome, NY	10,580	4
Springfield, MA	24,645	4
New Haven-Milford, CT	33,484	4
Portland-South Portland-Biddeford, ME	20,227	4
New York-Northern New Jersey-Long Island, NY-NJ-PA	750,407	4
Poughkeepsie-Newburgh-Middletown, NY	27,236	4

A 2012 study confirmed that the United States is no longer a Protestant-majority country. Adherents have dropped just below the 50 percent mark for the first time. Coupled with this shift in Protestant numbers is the rise of Americans stating they have no religious affiliation. Presently, 20 percent of all US adults (thirty-three million) comprise the quickly growing category of the "nones."[11] In all likelihood these demographic shifts reflect changes to come. Like the inching of a glacier that ever so slowly reshapes the land, changing faith systems are part of an ongoing sculpting process in the

United States. The country has now reached a tipping point in the numbers of those with little to no connection to a Judeo-Christian worldview.

Faiths on the Move

Of the 214 million international migrants in the world today, those who claim to be Christians make up 49 percent. Muslims comprise 27 percent, Hindus 5 percent, Buddhists 3 percent, and Jews 2 percent. Sikhs, Jains, Taoists, Chinese folk worshipers, and African traditional worshipers together comprise 4 percent.[12] As peoples move, they also bring their religious traditions with them. Hallal butchers increase their sales as the nations arrive in a midsized midwestern town. The temple increases weekly attendance in Munich as families arrive from India. School systems accommodate students needing to be absent for religious holidays other than Easter and Christmas.

North America and Europe receive a large percentage of these peoples on the move. The United States is the top destination for Buddhists and those with no religious affiliation. It is the second leading destination for Hindus and Jewish immigrants. It ranks seventh among destinations for Muslims, behind European nations such as Germany and France. The European Union is home to almost thirteen million Islamic immigrants, with Germany and France each having three million Muslims.[13]

Returning to the Apostolic[14]

I am a self-professed coffee snob. I am the guy who prefers coffee that is sold in the mom-and-pop microroasteries peppered across the United States. In fact I am writing this sentence while sitting in my favorite coffee shop in Birmingham. Six months ago when my family and I moved from Kentucky to Alabama, I started my quest for a good microroastery. After finding this one I started to brag to my friends that I had "discovered" a good coffee shop, only to learn some of them already knew about the place. The shop had been there for a few years. Many of the city's residents had been there already. I was not the first customer. I had not discovered anything. I simply started frequenting something that was already in place.

Effective mission in the West is going to require the church to return to a radically biblical approach to her labors. While healthy contextualization of the gospel is a must, it is not an attempt to repackage the gospel with more glitz and glamour. It is not an old product in search of a new way to reach its customer base. What is needed is a return to something that is two thousand years old. This return will cause many people to believe they have discovered something new, avant-garde, innovative, or creative. Nothing could be further from the truth. We need to frequent that which is already in place.

I recently spoke with a leader from a particular denomination. As we talked over coffee (at another coffee shop), he inquired about the direction of our church when it comes to church planting. I described our future missionary labors in terms of what we read in Acts 13–14; 16; 20; 1 Thessalonians 1:2–10; and Titus 1:5. He was surprised, as if my thoughts were coming from an unusual source. Unfortunately, over the years, I have found myself surprising many people during similar conversations. Whenever a biblical model for missions is viewed as unusual, the path to change will come with pain.

The challenge for the church in the West is not just how to think about her context as a missionary should think, but also how to act as a missionary would act in the shadow of dominant structures and organizations that are more pastoral in nature, birthed and developed within a Christian context of yesteryear. The return to apostolic or missionary thought and practice will be a great challenge for many churches. If the late twentieth century brought about "worship wars" among congregations, I can only speculate how such missional shifts will be received. In light of how poorly we (at least in the US) resist change, I believe few churches will make the necessary changes to reach the post-Christian West. Churches that are most likely to move forward effectively are those who embrace a radically biblical approach to sending missionary teams to function in apostolic ways when it comes to making disciples, planting churches, and appointing pastors in those churches. In order to better understand what I believe is necessary for approaching the West as a post-Christian mission field, it is helpful (with a history of Western Christianity in mind) to gain a brief glimpse of four shifts that seem to occur among a people once the gospel arrives in their context.

From Simplicity to Complexity

Typically when the gospel pioneers an area, the message, methods, and models used are simple in nature. Often the missionaries operate without much complexity. There is a desire to sow the gospel, teach the people simple obedience to the instructions of Jesus, and empower them to be the church among kith and kin. Such biblical simplicity helps foster the rapid dissemination of the gospel and the multiplication of disciples, leaders, and churches.

As the gospel continues to spread and the church matures, infrastructures, organizations, and methods tend to become more and more complex. What began as missionary activity with few elements beyond biblical simplicity develops into a highly structured paradigm for ministry and mission. Of course such development is not always a bad thing. It is a sociological reality that most organizations move from the simple to the complex. Sometimes such structures and organizations are necessary for healthy growth and development. Problems arise, however, when such complexity hinders the rapid dissemination of the gospel and the sanctification of the churches.

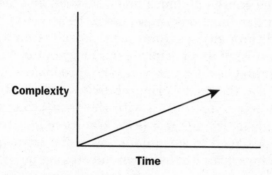

From Apostolic to Pastoral

A developing leadership is needed for a maturing church. Such is a good thing. What began as apostolic labors transitions to pastoral ministry for an established church among a people group:

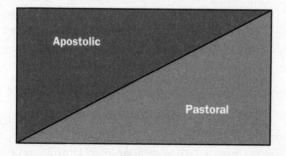

As the number of Christ followers increases within a society, the need for such missional engagement diminishes. The need for pastor-teachers (Eph. 4:11–12) to oversee the new churches to equip them to do the work of the ministry increases. People are no longer asking the Philippian jailer's question, "What must I do to be saved?" (Acts 16:30). Instead they ask, "How do we now live as followers of Jesus?"

From Apostolic Missiology to Pastoral Missiology

As the church becomes more pastoral and less apostolic in her functions, missions in that society become filtered through a pastoral lens instead of an apostolic lens, resulting in a pastoral missiology out of which the church then develops any ongoing missionary methods. Hopefully, those maturing churches will be reaching out to their communities with the gospel. Should they be evangelistic? Yes. However traditional, evangelistic labors designed to assimilate new believers into established churches with their own cultures are not sufficient if a sizable portion of the population requires missionary labors before people in the community will become kingdom citizens. What began in that society as missionary teams doing E-2 and E-3 (see chapter 1) church-planting labors results in the maturing churches beginning to do more and more E-0 and E-1 work as the lost population diminishes. However, if that society transitions (or never had a sizeable Christian population) whereby the need of the hour is once again E-2 or E-3, then change is required. Such is an extremely general summary of the history of missions and church growth in the West.

From Missionary Methods to Pastoral Methods

Our methods are derived from our missiology. If a community of believers shifts from a missiology that is apostolic in nature to a missiology that is pastoral in nature, then the evangelism, church planting, and leadership development methods will reflect such shifts as well. A result of a pastoral understanding of missions applied to a post-Christian context is generally not a failure to think and function missionally, but rather to think and function with a pastoral approach to missionary labors. Change has taken place, but for the most part churches continue in E-0 and E-1 efforts (primarily pastoral approaches) when E-2 and E-3 are desperately needed.

A pastoral missiology also leans toward maintenance and the conservation of structures and organizations. Such is the nature of pastoral ministry—even for many of the most evangelistic pastoral ministries—and it is a good thing for a pastor and an established local church. Pastors are called to be pastors. The heart of the pastor is rightly aligned in this direction for the sheep. Should missionaries be pastoral? Absolutely! Should pastors be apostolic? Absolutely! The Scriptures are clear on these matters. But whenever missionaries function primarily as pastors and pastors function primarily as missionaries, frustration and problems arise in the kingdom. Why? Because leaders are functioning outside of their callings and giftings. Missionaries and pastors are not the same creatures.

Need for Scaffolds

Unfortunately a pastoral missiology misapplies this good desire to the mission field, and it finds satisfaction in the planting of churches with believers who have been kingdom citizens for a long time rather than in recent converts from the harvest fields. A pastoral missiology typically wants to maintain and control rather than empower and release others to be and function as the local church in their context. By way of an old missiological analogy, a pastoral missiology understands missionaries to be like a scaffold, but desires that scaffold to remain attached to the building (that is, the local body of believers) once the construction is complete. An apostolic missiology recognizes the scaffold for what it is: something that is not a permanent fixture once the church has been planted. While the missionaries will continue to be involved in partnerships and leadership development with the newly planted churches and their pastors, they will refrain from membership in those churches.

Both/And

As long as a society has a large percentage of believers, a pastoral model may be sufficient for engaging the population. However, the boat of Western society has sailed deeply into post-Christian waters, so there is the need for both pastoral paradigms and a return to apostolic missionary teams. The church trying to operate with only one model is like a boat rowing against the tide with its anchor down. The church in the West, particularly in the United States and Canada, has been attempting such a nautical impossibility for a long time. The pastoral structures, models, and paradigms are well established in the West; the desperately needed apostolic ones are hardly in place.

As wise stewards of the mystery of Christ, we must understand biblical church planting as evangelism that results in new churches. Or, to communicate it in other terms, as disciple making that results in new churches. The weight of the biblical model is on this definition. Imagine what would happen if we created a church-planting atmosphere in the West where it is expected that new churches consist of 95–100 percent new believers at the moment those churches are planted. What would happen if our strategies did not embrace pastoral methods that instead yield new churches consisting of 95–100 percent long-term kingdom citizens at the moment of their births? What would happen if we used our Father's resources (be they money or people or time) to plant churches out of the harvest fields instead of creating a different style of worship and ministry for the believers who have been in the kingdom for many years?

The shifts in the Western world have created a pressure point on the church in a different way. Now she finds herself in a post-Christian context attempting to do ministry and mission as if the context were still the mid-twentieth century. The challenge is

1. to maintain the necessary pastoral responsibilities in light of a mature church comprised of long-term kingdom citizens,
2. to equip and commission apostolic bands to do evangelism that results in new churches, and
3. to raise up pastors from those churches.

A return to a Pauline approach to missionary labors is necessary but difficult since the church in the West now reads Acts and Paul's letters as if they were addressed to churches in contexts like ours. A fresh perspective is necessary when returning to the biblical text, one that recognizes Luke recorded the acts of apostolic bands and Paul wrote as a church planter to recently planted congregations.

Questions to Consider

1. Do you consider the West a post-Christian mission field? Unlike a field that has yet to receive the gospel, what do you think missions look like in a post-Christian area?
2. Is your church primarily engaged in E-0, E-1, E-2, or E-3 endeavors? Why? Is your work sufficient for the community? If not, what needs to change?
3. If your church is not regularly sending apostolic teams to plant churches, what needs to change so that this biblical practice may occur?

4. Were you surprised to learn that even in the United States there are states and urban contexts with such low numbers of evangelicals? How can you share this information with your church so that it may lead to the sending of apostolic teams to those areas as church planters?

3

Growth of the Majority World Church

It is like a grain of mustard seed, which, when sown on the ground, is the smallest of all the seeds on earth, yet when it is sown it grows up and becomes larger than all the garden plants and puts out large branches, so that the birds of the air can make nests in its shade.

—MARK 4:31–32

One of the most influential individuals on my ministry and thoughts regarding church multiplication is Charles Brock. Charles and his wife, Dottie, served as missionaries in the Philippines for twenty years, planting networks of churches.[1] When I first met Charles, he had returned from the Philippines and was overseeing his own church-planting training ministry, Church Growth International. I have heard Charles share many great stories of how the Spirit worked in the Philippines, bringing people into the kingdom. Several years after meeting Charles, I had the honor of getting to know Sadiri Joy Tira, Filipino-Canadian missiologist and author of *Filipino Kingdom Workers*. I am always thrilled to hear Joy share stories of the multitudes of Filipinos now venturing across the world into the Middle East, North Africa, and Asia as tentmakers, making disciples and planting churches as they work with their hands in the marketplace.

Charles and Joy represent what the Spirit has been doing throughout the Majority World.[2] The Spirit sent many from the West, and through their sacrifices not only has a great harvest come but also the maturing church is sending its members to the unreached peoples of the world. The gospel did not stop with Charles, and now it is not stopping with men such as Joy and other Filipinos.

An *Enquiry* into the Majority World Church

It was the late eighteenth century, and a young Englishman had developed a passion for reaching the nations with the gospel. Many during his day did not share his newfound zeal. During one particular meeting in which he attempted to make the case for the evangelization of the nations, someone in attendance admonished him with the now infamous words, "Sit down young man. If God wants to save the heathen, he will do so without using you or me."

This young man was William Carey, and he would shortly thereafter publish in 1792 a brief book with the title *An Enquiry into the Obligation of Christians to Use Means for the Conversion of the Heathens*. This work, challenging the church to send missionaries across the world to preach the gospel through a missionary society, would lead to the formation of the Baptist Missionary Society and the launch of the modern Protestant missions movement. While others such as the Moravians had gone before Carey, the next two centuries would experience a significant surge in Protestant missionaries departing from England and America to make disciples in many of the countries of the world.

During this period the gospel would take root, peoples would come to faith in Jesus, and churches would be planted. Just as North Americans and Western Europeans heard the calls to follow Jesus and go into all the world, the results of two centuries of Protestant missionary labors have now resulted in those believers in

Africa, Latin America, and Asia now going into all the world to share the gospel. Today the largest number of Christ followers live outside of the Western world, and the fastest church growth is occurring there too.

Some local churches outside of the West have grown into some of the largest in the world and have complex organizations. Just as in the West, time and complexity has brought conflict and controversy. Nigeria is a case in point. Protestant missionaries began laboring in the early nineteenth century, and by the twenty-first century evangelicals comprised 31 percent of the population.[3] As I wrote this chapter, *Christianity Today* published an article noting that one of the latest problems is the fact that Nigerian Pentecostal preachers are having to defend their rights to own private jets so they can speed up the process of evangelization.[4] While my point is not to draw attention to problems among the churches in Nigeria, the fact such a debate makes headlines is a revelation of how far—at times much to her chagrin—the church has come since the nineteenth century.

Presently, Nigeria claims to be 51 percent Christian, with evangelicals comprising 31 percent of the 158 million people. Despite the ecclesiastical problems, the kingdom citizens who reside in Nigeria have been involved in some of the world's largest known prayer movements. Rapid church growth has been taking place among Anglicans, Methodists, Presbyterians, Baptists, Pentecostals, Charismatics, and other evangelical groups. It was during the 1970s that many Nigerian students caught the vision for global missions that resulted in a movement of over five thousand missionaries now serving at home and abroad.[5]

Recently I was introduced to a young Korean pastor who was visiting Birmingham to participate in a disciple-making conference that our senior pastor, David Platt, and Francis Chan were hosting. It was made known that our new Korean friend was the pastor of a seventy-thousand-member congregation! While the growth of the church in

South Korea has been studied for years, many of us living in the Western world often forget the miracle behind this growth and the fact that the largest church in the world is in Korea with over eight hundred thousand members. The first American Protestant missionaries arrived in the country in the late nineteenth century; the first Protestant church was planted in 1884. Korea experienced a Great Awakening in the first decade of the twentieth century. One hundred years later, the world looks at the church in South Korea as an example in many ways. It is now estimated that fifty thousand Korean churches exist, and over twenty thousand missionaries have been sent to the nations. This makes South Korea one of the largest missionary-sending countries in the world.[6]

Consider the following points Mark A. Noll made in his book, *The New Shape of World Christianity*. His comparisons of the Majority World realities and those in the West are bittersweet. While many unhealthy things have been occurring in the churches in the Western world, Noll's observations nevertheless are encouraging reminders of the power of the gospel in the Majority World.

- In all likelihood, more believers gathered for worship in China than in all of "Christian Europe."
- More Anglicans gathered for worship this past Sunday in each of Kenya, South Africa, Tanzania, and Uganda than the Anglicans gathering in Britain and Canada, and Episcopalians in the United States combined.
- More Presbyterians gathered for worship this past Sunday in Ghana than in Scotland.
- There were six to eight times as many people gathering for worship in the Yoido Full Gospel Church in Seoul as gathered for worship in Canada's ten largest churches.
- Europe's largest church is in Kiev and is pastored by a Nigerian of Pentecostal background.

- Each week fifteen thousand missionaries, mostly from Africa and Asia, are evangelizing communities in Great Britain.[7]

The centers for much Christian activity are found in Africa, Asia, and Latin America. It has been estimated that by 2025 the world will contain 2.6 billion Christians, with 633 million from Africa, 640 million from Latin America, 460 million from Asia, and 555 million from Europe.[8] The Pew Forum on Religion and Public Life notes that the evangelical Protestant percentage in the United States is 26 percent.[9] When compared to some of the other countries in the world, we quickly realize that other nations exceed us in this area.

Select Countries with Evangelical Percentages[10]

Country	Evangelical Percentage
Kenya	49%
Uganda	37%
Central African Republic	32%
El Salvador	32%
Zimbabwe	31%
Nigeria	31%
Nicaragua	30%
Burundi	27%

Forgetting About the Mustard Seed

I do not believe that the majority of the churches in the Western world realize what the Lord has been doing across the globe. I grew up in a missions-minded denomination. Missions education was prevalent, even in our churches that were doing very little when it came to missions. However, I was long into my adult years before I heard people talking about the growth of the gospel in the Majority World, and such discussions were not happening in the churches but in the academy among missiologists. For over two hundred years we sacrificed and sent people to share, but we never asked the question, "What did God do as a result of our going?" We should not be surprised at the gracious hand of the Lord in and through our missionary activities. After all, He has promised to gather peoples from all the nations in His throne room (Rev. 7:9). Rather, we should be surprised at our failure to understand and communicate such great matters to our churches in the West. When planted, the mustard seed is small and is easily overlooked, but how could we hide the reality that the seed grew and developed into a massive plant with large branches?

Not only has the gospel spread rapidly throughout the world, but it has resulted in numerous churches sending out their own missionaries. For those of us who have only heard the story that we must go and make disciples, as if there were no disciples in such countries, we are shocked whenever we read how many missionaries come from the Majority World.

Select Missionary-Sending Countries[11]

Country	Missionaries
India	82,950
China, PRC	20,000
Nigeria	6,644
Philippines	4,500
Indonesia	3,000
Ghana	2,000
Ukraine	1,599
Mexico	794
Bangladesh	500
Thailand	468
Malaysia	380
Argentina	350
Japan	300
Romania	130

While such growth does not release churches in the West from going into all the world, we must recognize that many of the countries of the world now receiving missionaries are also simultaneously sending missionaries. This is great! The Spirit of conversion is also the Spirit of mission. This present reality is a reminder that a lengthy period of time is not necessary before a new follower of Jesus should become involved in making disciples of all nations (Mark 5:1–20; Acts 9:20).

Thailand is one example of the work of the missionary Spirit of God. As of 1982, only a couple of Thai missionaries were known to be serving outside of Thailand. Edwin Zehner noted that a couple of years later, churches were seriously considering sending missionaries to other countries. And by 2007 several pastors were openly discussing such work, with many of them having members already going on short-term teams abroad. By the beginning of the twenty-first century, Thailand was a missionary-sending country while still existing as primarily a missionary-receiving country. Less than 1 percent of the population consists of Christians, and one thousand missionaries were registered as serving in the country as of 2007.[12]

Opportunities for Mission

The growth of the bride of Christ in the Majority World is cause for much celebration. There is no country on earth where followers of Jesus do not exist. Of course, as noted in chapter 1, reaching a geopolitical nation-state is not the same thing as reaching "all nations," as Jesus commanded us in Matthew 28:19. While the gospel has brought about fruit for the kingdom, there are several important practical matters for Western churches and mission agencies to keep in mind in light of this great global working of the Spirit.

Partnerships, Not Abandonment

While the word *partnership* has been commonly used to describe the desired relationships between churches in the West with the Majority World for gospel advancement, I am not certain that enough churches are considering this opportunity and the components necessary for such relationships. Two hundred years of Protestant paternalistic missionary work—not to mention the centuries of paternalistic Catholic service—has the potential to create defensiveness among those in the Majority World and a hands-off approach from those in the West. When this defensiveness is coupled with the rugged individualism found among citizens of the United States, partnership often becomes a great challenge.

I have participated in conferences in which Majority World church leaders have been present and have clearly made known the wounds they still carry from generations of missionaries functioning in a paternalistic manner over their forefathers. Though those errors are from days long ago, their effects are still felt on the contemporary generations. What is done today has ramifications on the future.

We should not be surprised whenever we approach Majority World believers with good intentions for partnerships for gospel advancement and they respond with a suspicious attitude toward us. For years Western governments exploited many of the nations of the world for their natural resources and people. This continues with Western corporations. Promises have been made, only to be broken at a later date. History records partnerships between corporations and governments that have benefited the few at the expense of the majority. Our brothers and sisters have a right to be cautious and discerning whenever we approach them regarding partnerships. We must be patient and sensitive to this matter and commend them for their wisdom.

However, there are those in the West, desiring to avoid the paternalistic problems of yesteryear, who take a laissez-faire approach to partnership. Rather than being an active participant, they give up all responsibilities to make disciples of all nations by allowing national believers to do all of the work. This is not a healthy way to approach partnerships either.

During one gathering I attended of church leaders from both the Western and Majority Worlds, much of what was communicated was that missionaries from the West had made many mistakes on the mission field and, therefore, should get out of the way and allow the Majority World churches to take over and be in charge. It was declared that the church in the West was dead and had little to contribute to gospel advancement today in the Majority World. Needless to say, I was very upset when I left this gathering.

The problems of the past coupled with the growth of Majority World churches sometimes foster such attitudes among church leaders today. While the practical result of such attitudes can manifest in different ways, one such way is that the West should simply send money to churches in other parts of the world and allow them to do the work. While I recognize the value of Majority World believers reaching their own neighbors, the truth is that the Great Commission of Jesus is just as binding on Western churches as it is on Majority World churches. For those of us in the West to abdicate our missionary labors among the nations is a direct violation of the call of Christ on our lives. The growth of the Majority World church is not an excuse for us to fail to go and make disciples. As noted in chapter 1, there are still thousands of unreached and unengaged peoples across the world. Just as Jesus has called us to walk in obedience in other areas of our lives, we are called to go, preach, and teach.

Partnership is not always possible, and oftentimes those closest to the field—physically and culturally—do not make the best decisions about missions. Just look to many churches in the West for examples of this reality. However, where churches exist in other parts of the world, it is important for missionaries from other churches to work in partnership with them as much as it is possible. This is absolutely not a call for doctrinal, missiological, or philosophical compromise but an opportunity for kingdom synergism whereby more is accomplished working together than working separately.

While we addressed the matter of the West as a mission field in chapter 2, here it is important to recognize that missionaries are being sent to the West to make disciples in these post-Christian lands. The arrival of such brothers and sisters provides another opportunity for partnerships. While attending a missions conference in England, South African-born Shaun Pillay sensed the Lord leading him to go to the United States to plant churches. The exact location would be in Connecticut, a state with a 4 percent evangelical presence. Southern Baptists in the United States entered into partnerships with Shaun and his wife, Deshni; and while ministering in Norwich, the Pillays planted Cornerstone Bible Church.[13]

One of my students from Nepal caught the vision for working with the Bhutanese pastors who had been resettled in the United States as refugees. He, along with church leaders in the United States, began to gather these men together to cast the vision before them to make disciples and plant churches in their new homeland. He has started a network of several Nepali-Bhutanese pastors and churches across this country. It is also observed that many African immigrants, upon arriving in the United States, have experienced a call to plant churches here.[14]

What We Can Learn

There is much to learn from our brothers and sisters scattered throughout the world. In fact, the brevity of this chapter will not permit me to even come close to exhausting a list. Regardless, I want to draw our attentions to a few matters. While I do not wish to write a hagiography, I do believe that if Hebrews 11 was written today, it would also be filled with many contemporary examples from the Majority World. So what can we in the West learn from them?

First, in general, the church in the Majority World is a theologically conservative body. There is a high view of the Bible as the Word of God. It is respected and not demythologized, deconstructed, or denigrated. The conservative theological convictions appealed so much to the Anglican Church in North America that they withdrew from fellowship with the liberal Episcopal Church in the United States and the Anglican Church of Canada and affiliated with the church of Rwanda, desiring oversight and spiritual care from the churches in Africa.

While theological differences exist, the West has much to learn from the Majority World when it comes to the value of the Bible for both faith and life. Over the years, theological liberalism, neoorthodoxy, and postmodern interpretations have eroded many of the foundations of historical orthodox Christian beliefs. The Majority World churches in belief and practice share more in common with the first-century believers than they do with many Christians in the West.

Second, and closely connected to their respect for orthodoxy, there is much to learn from their convictions regarding the reality of the supernatural in everyday life. While I am not advocating that we embrace animistic beliefs that have crept into the church in the Majority World, I am attempting to draw us back to a right belief in the existence of God and miracles, demons and spiritual warfare, and signs and wonders that sometimes accompany the preaching of the gospel to the lost. Also, it should be noted that neither am I attempting to call us to return to some of the erroneous ways of the signs-and-wonders movement or prosperity theology. However, the Bible speaks often on these matters, and the Western church has often wed too much of the scientific worldview and anti-supernatural bias to the Bible to create a Westernized syncretistic Christianity that is not true to the Scriptures.

Third, our brothers and sisters in the Majority World remind us of the simplicity of the faith. At the end of its first three centuries, Christianity became one of the officially recognized religions, and it accomplished this feat with few material resources. While there are exceptions, the Majority World believers are accomplishing more for gospel advancement with little more than God's Word and His Spirit than the church in the West is accomplishing with all of our money, organizations, and structures. They are an example to us that faith can be vibrant and the church both simple and dynamic.

Fourth, whenever we turn our attentions to the Majority World, we often observe faith under fire. The persecution and opposition that many are presently experiencing is unlike anything the West has seen in centuries. Some of these churches know what it is like to be tested for the kingdom and persecuted for righteousness' sake (Matt. 5:10–11). They relate to the martyrs under the altar who cry out to the Lord, "How long?" (Rev. 6:9–11). They have much to teach us about life and mission in the context of violence.

Finally, they remind us that even within such difficult circumstances we are to sacrifice for the mission of the King. The spirit of the original Moravian missionaries is alive and well among many churches throughout the Majority World. As they go in search of work and education, they also go with a message. Africans are sacrificing much to take the gospel into Europe. Filipinos living in diaspora are intentionally seeking out jobs across the globe, not only to make a living, but to be on mission. Rather than waiting for money to arrive or a mission agency to accept and send them, many Korean and Chinese churches are doing what they can to send their peoples to the Middle East as tentmakers.

How We Can Help

We have all heard the saying, "The grass is always greener on the other side of the fence." So, lest I be accused of elevating the status of the Majority World church to a plane that does not exist in reality or appear to be denigrating the church in the West, I want to draw our attentions to what we can also contribute to partnership with kingdom citizens in the non-Western world. Not everything happening in the Majority World is good and healthy. There are numerous examples of false teachings and unhealthy ministries. Again, for the sake of space, I am only able to mention a few matters where I believe we can contribute much value.

First, Protestant church history in the Majority World is somewhat brief in time. The West has had more time to experience both good and bad examples that the Majority World can learn from as they live on mission in the days to come. Missions history is a very important subject that should be taught to younger churches. Good kingdom stewardship demands that the wheel of progress not be reinvented and potholes of devastation be avoided at all costs. Understanding one's past is a means to more faithful service.

Second, zeal without knowledge is not a good thing, for the one who makes haste will miss the way (Prov. 19:2). While I am grateful for the enthusiasm and sacrificial lifestyles of many throughout the world, some believers and churches have little to no equipping for ministry and mission. I am not advocating that the West export centuries of seminary structure and organization onto our brothers and sisters. Unfortunately, many are doing just this—often at the request of the Majority World. After fourteen years of being a professor in US classrooms, I am not convinced we are getting theological education right here, so let's not export it there.

The West has much knowledge and experience that if communicated in a humble, respectful, and contextually appropriate way that is local-church based could strengthen churches across the world. Rather than export models and methods to the Majority World, the West needs to equip them in not only understanding how to study the Bible, but how to think as kingdom citizens and apply principles for life, ministry, and mission in their contexts. False teachings spread like wildfire across China and parts of Africa. Pastors do not know how to respond to some challenges to the truth of Christ. The ability to walk alongside others to assist them in becoming equipped for every good work is not only a critical need in the world today, but one that the West can assist in with little effort.

Third, while there is much missionary activity in the Majority World, there is not enough of it. I periodically hear stories from Majority World church leaders of how their people groups have the gospel but have not caught the vision to take that message across cultures to other unreached people groups. In the 1970s the church in Indonesia was one example of this matter. There was a large Christian presence in this heavily Muslim-populated nation. Many of the Indonesian churches were inwardly focused, doing little to reach the large numbers of unreached peoples living on the nearby islands.

Thankfully, change has been occurring among some churches as a result of obtaining a vision for their neighbors. I have been told by Haitian and Nigerian church leaders of the need for a Great Commission vision among the churches in their countries. Across the world, those of us in the West can help Majority World church leaders cast vision for making disciples of all nations. Walking hand in hand with some churches will be necessary when it comes to modeling the apostolic work of church planting. While avoiding paternalism, we need to consider—with much prayer—Paul's words to the churches he exhorted to imitate him as he imitated Christ (1 Cor. 11:1). Wouldn't it be wonderful to be able to assist other churches in imitating us as we imitate Christ and then to see the word of the Lord ringing forth from them (1 Thess. 1:6–8)?

* * *

The most rapid church growth today is occurring in the Majority World. The largest numbers of Christ followers live outside of the Western countries. Many Majority World churches are now sending missionaries across the globe, including to Western countries. While the growth of the Majority World church is a good thing for the body of Christ, such rapid growth comes with challenges. The need for healthy biblical teaching and leadership development is a common cry from such church leaders. Also churches in the West, with their large amounts of material resources, education, and skilled leaders, need to consider how they can partner with such Majority World Christians for the advancement of the gospel. Issues such as pride, racism, competition, and paternalism are among some of the challenges that will interfere with healthy partnerships.

Questions to Consider

1. Is it a surprise to you that there are so many Christians among the nations today? If so, why? If you have not heard of the growth of the church in the Majority World until now, why do you think such is the case?

2. Are you and your church ready to cast the vision before Majority World Christians living in your community to work with you to make disciples and plant churches? Will you help equip such believers for this great task?

3. What do you anticipate will be the greatest challenges to your church as you attempt to work with churches in the Majority World?

4. What are the greatest strengths that your church has to assist churches in the Majority World for the advancement of the gospel?

5. What can you and your church learn from Majority World believers?

4

Pluralism and the Plurality of Faiths

I am the way. . . . No one comes to the Father except through me.

—John 14:6

Religion is alive and well across the globe in the twenty-first century and remains a pressure point on the church and her mission. As I write this chapter today, President Barak Obama is being sworn in for his second term in office. There was media coverage on the Bibles of Abraham Lincoln and Martin Luther King Jr. on which Obama placed his hand and swore his oath.[1] Last year, an anti-Islam video was released online leading to violent outbursts in many countries including Egypt, Yemen, Sudan, Libya, Indonesia, Afghanistan, and Pakistan. The prophecies of yesteryear heralding the day when religion would give way to an anti-supernatural, anti-god worldview have long since come to pass. Neither science nor government nor materialism has removed or diminished the effect of religion from the nations of this world. People have always been—and always will be—on a quest to quiet their restless hearts. The extensive destructive nature of sin has resulted in wanderers who will continue to wander until they find peace in Christ alone.

And while such wanderings have resulted in the development of religious ideologies, systems, and organizations, they have also brought the world to a new point in history. Coupled with globalization (see chapter 6), the flames of religion are felt around the globe, and the world knows it. A small-church pastor in Florida can just threaten to burn the Qur'an, and the pope (in Rome) and the president (in Washington) are moved to action requesting that such an act not occur. Why? Because the threat alone resulted in public protests in Pakistan and Afghanistan. When the actual desecration of the book occurred, people were killed in Kabul.

I was once attempting to witness to a girl sitting next to me in a coffee shop in Indianapolis. I quickly found out that she was "spiritual," for she was very excited to have had the chance to hear a public presentation by the Dalai Lama in a nearby city. Here was a non-Buddhist girl interested in hearing from a man who is the representation of an expression of Buddhism—a living world religion.

Sarah and I once vacationed in Muskegon, Michigan. We stayed at a bed-and-breakfast with a very gracious host. I noticed that she had a copy of the Qur'an on a desk near the front door. On the day we were checking out, I inquired about the book on the desk and quickly found out that she had been a Baptist, was trying to follow the teachings of the Nation of Islam, and frequently watched Creflo Dollar's television programs!

Pluralism: How the Pressure Is Felt—Internally

The influence and growth of faith traditions today apply pressure on the church from at least two angles. First, there is the internal pressure. The church is able to experience the faiths of the world in ways unlike generations before us. Al Jazeera, CNN, Facebook, Twitter, and YouTube provide us with instantaneous news related to the Arab Spring and bombings in India. Many people across the world began to inquire about the beliefs of Sikhism when the media brought to our attention the horrific murders that took place when a gunman opened fire in a Sikh temple in Wisconsin in 2012.[2]

And coupled with the media, the church is exposed to the migration of the nations unlike any time in history (see chapter 5). It is common to find numerous streets across the Western world where several faith traditions are represented among the residents who live there. Children from Christian homes go to school and play with children from the homes of Taoist, Shinto, agnostic, and Muslim families.

And while such diversity should encourage us to share the love and hope that is found in Jesus, a typical result is that the church begins to make comparisons with those around her and not comparisons to a holy God:

> "Those people are more devout than I am. Can my way be the right way?"
>
> "He is a nice man and dearly loves his family. His faith is more transforming than mine."
>
> "She is a great person to hang out with and very moral. I wish I could control my temper as she does."
>
> "How can I call such people to repent and place faith in Jesus? Maybe all that I have heard is not correct. Maybe there is another way, likely many ways."
>
> "There has to be another way. How dare I say that I am right and everyone else is wrong. That is not tolerant. Too narrow-minded. A God of love would never be like that."

And so the deception continues on an internal level, with the church listening to a still small voice asking, "Did God actually say . . . ?" (Gen. 3:1).

I was once in one of my favorite Chinese restaurants when I noticed that one of the servers was taking his lunch break and eating at one of the tables. As I returned to my table from the buffet, I noticed that this Chinese man was praying over his food with hands folded and head bowed. I was very impressed that he was not only giving thanks before his meal, but also very open in his expression. Upon another trip to get some more General Tso's chicken, I stopped to encourage this man. I told him that I could not help but notice that he prayed over his meal, and I inquired if he was a follower of Jesus. "Oh yes, I am!"

His response was very encouraging, so I inquired as to what church he was a member of in the area, and upon hearing his answer I asked him how long he had been a follower of the Lord. "Since I came to America," he replied. "I married an American woman and became a Christian." But before I could offer a word of encouragement, he shared with me some most discouraging information. "When I am in America, I am a Christian, but when I return overseas, I become a Buddhist." General Tso's chicken did not taste as good after our conversation.

This man's words reveal pluralism in action. While this pressure point does not always reveal itself among people shifting back and forth among faith traditions like a chameleon changing according to its environment, the worldview is widespread, particularly in the West. Pluralism, as related to salvation, is the view that there are many paths to God. Jesus is understood to be one way among many, but not the only way. God is seen as not being exclusive; rather He allows people to devise a multitude of possible faith traditions in order to obtain eternal paradise.

A close companion to this understanding of salvation is inclusivism. This view is the belief that Jesus is the only way, but people come to the Father through different means. Abiding by the pillars of Islam is one way. The way of the Buddha is another. Regardless, the sacrifice of Jesus on the cross for the forgiveness of sins is required, but it is just that people—especially those who have never heard of Jesus—come to God as best they know how, but without faith in Jesus. In a glob-alized and multicultural world, one of the challenges facing the church is connected to the question, is Jesus the only way to God? Many in the Western world would say absolutely not.[3] Many within the church hold to the views of pluralism or inclusivism as well.

There are several reasons why such is unfortunate. First and foremost, the overwhelming biblical support from Genesis to Revelation is that the God of Abraham, Isaac, Jacob, the nation of Israel, and the first-century believers is an exclusive God. There are no gods before Him or after Him (Isa. 43:10). And among the so-called gods of the nations surrounding the Israel-ites in the Old Testament, He refers to them as false gods (Jer. 14:22). He calls the nations to come to Him, through exclusive means as delineated in the first five books of the Old Testament. As His plan of salvation history unfolds, we come to see that in the fullness of time He incarnates Himself among His fallen creation (John 1:1; Gal. 4:4). He calls tax collectors (Matt. 9:10), religious devotees (John 3:1–3), and Samaritans (John 4:10) to repentance and faith. Jesus was explicit in that He is the only way to God (John 14:6). The first-century believers declared to very religious Jews that salva-tion is only in Jesus (Acts 4:12). Paul called Jews and Gentiles to repentance and faith (Acts 20:21) as well as polytheistic Athenians (Acts 17:22–34). Peter shared the way of Jesus with religious pilgrims who were prac-ticing their faith in Jerusalem (Acts 2:38–39) and also devout God-fearers (Acts 10:34–43). Paul's letter to the Roman believers clearly describes the fallen nature of all people, their separation from God, and the fact that no one seeks God (Rom. 3:10–11). Confession that Jesus is Lord and belief in one's heart that He was raised from the dead is an absolute necessity for salvation (Rom. 10:9). Jesus warns us that passionate religiosity is not sufficient for having one's name written in the Book of Life (Matt. 7:21–23).

Second, the views of pluralism and inclusivism hinder the apostolic work of the church. Biblical doctrine is the fuel for mission. Without right belief, especially about God and the salvation of people, the notion of making disciples of all nations is a practice in futility.

For years, I have been driving my vehicle with a broken gas gauge. Sometimes the needle is on *E* when I have a half tank of gas, and sometimes the display reveals a half tank of gas when it is actually empty. I have learned to drive by resetting my trip odometer each time I fill up with gas. I know that whenever my odometer reads within a certain range of miles, it is time to make a pit stop. Such was a good practice . . . when I lived in an area that was very flat. Upon moving to Birmingham where it is hilly in places, my vehicle required more fuel to cover the terrain. My odometer did not change with the topography; however, the amount of fuel required to drive within my "range of miles" did change. Couple this factor with a constant use of the air conditioner, and over the course of two weeks, I ran out of fuel. Twice!

Just as a car will not move forward without the proper fuel, the church that does not believe in the exclusive nature of Jesus' atonement on the cross and the necessity for people to put explicit faith in Him halts gospel advancement. Why should anyone risk life and limb, financial resources, and time if Jesus is not the only way to the Father? Missions would be foolish. According to the logic of inclusivism, we should never share the gospel with others, lest we send them to hell. Imagine how evil it would be to share Christ with someone who then rejects the truth of the good news after this revelation has been made known to him or her. Following this perspective, our preaching and their rejection has now damned them to hell. It would have been better to keep our mouths shut and allow them to wander into eternity in their ignorance—if God would save them simply because they did the best with what they knew.

Plurality of Faiths: How the Pressure Is Felt—Externally

The second way the pressure is felt is by the obvious growth of faith traditions and their resistance to the gospel. This external force has less to do with the theological question, Is Jesus the only Savior? and more to do with the church living in a multireligious, flat world, knowing Jesus is the only Savior.

Global Religious Diversity

Like the scattering of a dandelion's seeds in the wind, the movement of the peoples of this world across the centuries has widely diffused their religions. Explorations, trade routes, business, colonization, missionary activities, wars, disasters, and education have contributed to the dispersion of these faith traditions, so much so that adherents are often residing far beyond

10 Largest Concentrations of Select Religious Traditions as of 2010[4]

Folk Religionists		Hindus	
Country	Pop.	Country	Pop.
China	294,320,000	India	973,750,000
Vietnam	39,750,000	Nepal	24,170,000
Taiwan	10,260,000	Bangladesh	13,520,000
India	5,840,000	Indonesia	4,050,000
Brazil	5,540,000	Pakistan	3,330,000
South Sudan	3,270,000	Sri Lanka	2,830,000
North Korea	3,010,000	United States	1,790,000
Burma (Myanmar)	2,760,000	Malaysia	1,720,000
Burkina Faso	2,530,000	Burma (Myanmar)	820,000
Nigeria	2,290,000	United Kingdom	800,000
	World Total		**World Total**
	405,120,000		1,033,080,000

the geographical origins of the religion. For example, Baha'i has origins in Iran, but the largest concentrations of its five to seven million adherents are in India and the United States.[5] Though Islam began in Saudi Arabia, Indonesia is the country with the largest number of Muslims.

The table below shows where the largest populations of folk religionists, Hindus, Buddhists, and practitioners of other religions are located in the world. Folk religionists adhere to faith systems often unique to a particular people or tribe such as that of Native Americans, Aborigines, or Chinese Folk Religions. The category of other religions includes many of the world's smaller religions such as Shintoism, Taoism, Zoroastrianism, Jainism, Sikism, Wicca, and Baha'i to name a few. Because the numbers of Muslims and those subscribing to no religion at all have been growing, I have decided to address these categories separately in this chapter.

Buddhists		Jews		Others	
Country	Pop.	Country	Pop.	Country	Pop.
China	244,130,000	United States	5,690,000	India	27,560,000
Thailand	64,420,000	Israel	5,610,000	China	9,080,000
Japan	45,820,000	Canada	350,000	Japan	5,890,000
Burma (Myanmar)	38,410,000	France	310,000	Taiwan	3,760,000
Sri Lanka	14,450,000	United Kingdom	280,000	North Korea	3,130,000
Vietnam	14,380,000	Germany	230,000	United States	1,900,000
Cambodia	13,690,000	Russia	230,000	Cameroon	530,000
South Korea	11,050,000	Argentina	200,000	Kenya	500,000
India	9,250,000	Australia	110,000	United Kingdom	500,000
Malaysia	5,010,000	Brazil	110,000	Singapore	490,000
World Total 487,540,000		**World Total** 13,850,000		**World Total** 58,110,000	

This table is another reminder of the challenge that the world's faith traditions present against the spread of the gospel. Of course, this challenge is nothing new. Long ago, Paul noted that the god of this age has blinded the minds of people to the gospel (2 Cor. 4:4). While humanitarian good can be found among those who subscribe to such traditions, such faith is not representative of the saving faith that a holy and loving God expects. A glimpse at these numbers—and those to come—should move us to prayer and service as we recognize the enormity of the challenge in seeing the nations come to adore their Creator.

Growth of Islam

Yet these numbers are only part of the larger religious puzzle in the world today. Islam is the second largest world religion. Much attention has been given to it since 9/11. It is already the fastest-growing religion in the United States and Europe, and with such rapid growth (mainly through birth rates and immigration), more discussions are likely to occur in days to come.

Islam has been a subject of recent study by the Pew Research Center's Forum on Religion and Public Life.[6] Presently, the global Muslim population is around 1.6 billion people, with the majority living in the Asia-Pacific region. This number is expected to swell by 35 percent in the next couple of decades to 2.2 billion people. This growth rate—while slower than in the previous two decades—is almost twice the projected growth of the global non-Muslim population. By 2030, it is expected that Muslims will comprise over 26 percent of the world's population, including almost 30 percent of all fifteen- to twenty-nine-year-olds:

Countries with the Largest Muslim Populations 2010, 2030[7]

Country	2010 Pop. (millions)	Country	Est. 2030 Pop. (millions)
Indonesia	205	Pakistan	256
Pakistan	178	Indonesia	239
India	177	India	236
Bangladesh	149	Bangladesh	188
Egypt	80	Nigeria	117
Nigeria	76	Egypt	105
Iran	75	Iran	90
Turkey	75	Turkey	89
Algeria	35	Afghanistan	51
Morocco	32	Iraq	48

Births and migration will continue to fuel the growth. By 2030 it is expected that the United States will be home to over 6 million Muslims (2.6 million in 2010), a number more than any European country other than Russia and France. During this same time, the number is expected to triple in Canada to almost 2.7 million. The European population is projected to increase by one-third in the next two decades, bringing the number to over 58 million Muslims. The following table shows a comparison of the present Muslim portion with the estimated number in 2030, in selected countries and regions.

2010, 2030 Comparison of Muslim Proportions by Selected Countries and Regions[8]

Country/Region	Percent of pop. 2010	Percent of pop. 2030
Austria	5.7	9.3
Belgium	6	10.2
Canada	2.8	6.6
France	7.5	10.3
Israel	17.7	23.2
Sweden	4.9	9.9
United Kingdom	4.6	8.2
United States	0.8	1.7
Asia-Pacific	24.8	27.3
Sub-Saharan Africa	29.6	31
Europe	6	8

Patrick Johnstone, in his excellent book *The Future of the Global Church: History, Trends, and Possibilities*, notes that reports continue to flow from countries across the world of the spread of the gospel among Muslims. During the middle of the twentieth century, the church began seeing more and more Muslims coming to faith in Jesus. Persecution is often present for believers in countries such as Indonesia, Nigeria, Bangladesh, Algeria, Kazakhstan, and Sudan. And countries such as Iran and Saudi Arabia have an official death penalty for apostasy. Regardless, the Holy Spirit has been doing some amazing work in some of the most challenging locations and peoples in the world. Due to the sensitivity of the work, reports are sometimes difficult to obtain, but Johnstone notes that the following conservative 2005 estimates offer us an exciting glimpse of the advancement of the gospel among Muslim background peoples.

Global Estimates of Muslim Background Believers, 2005[9]

Country	Est. Muslim Background Believers, 2005
Indonesia	6,000,000
Nigeria	500,000
Iran	500,000
Ethiopia	400,000
United States	300,000
Burkina Faso	200,000
Tanzania	150,000
Bangladesh	130,000
Algeria	100,000
Cameroon	80,000
Kenya	70,000
Ghana	50,000
Saudi Arabia	50,000
Benin	40,000
Bulgaria	40,000
Canada	40,000
Uganda	30,000
Kazakhstan	25,000
Sudan	25,000
United Kingdom	20,000
World Total	8,970,000

The "Nones"

The pressure of plurality raises the number of people who do not adhere to any official world religion. One in every five adults in the United States is in the category of the religiously unaffiliated, including one-third of all adults under the age of thirty. The Nones include thirteen million declared atheists and agnostics as well as thirty-three million with no religious affiliation. It should be noted that religious practices such as prayer and religious beliefs in the supernatural do exist among those who subscribe to no affiliation.[10]

On a global scale, the number of those who claim no religious affiliation exceeds one billion. Nations historically known for communist ideology and secular strongholds still contain some of the largest concentrations of such peoples.

Countries with the Largest Number of Religiously Unaffiliated[11]

Country	Estimated Population
China	700,680,000
Japan	72,120,000
United States	50,980,000
Vietnam	26,040,000
Russia	23,180,000
South Korea	22,350,000
Germany	20,350,000
France	17,580,000
North Korea	17,350,000
Brazil	15,410,000
Total Found in All Countries	1,126,500,000

Contextualization Matters

The pressure point of pluralism and the plurality of faiths across the world reveals the necessity for the church to understand her context as she takes the love of Jesus to the nations. Understanding a people geographically, demographically, culturally, spiritually, politically, historically, and linguistically helps us to understand how best to communicate the gospel, make disciples, plant churches, teach obedience, and raise up leadership for those churches. The numbers listed in this chapter only provide a glimpse of what is occurring across the world. The best way to understand the people whom you are called to serve is to get to know them. While it is helpful to know that eighty million Muslims reside in Egypt and that we should study Islam so as to better understand the Egyptians, the true realities of life and culture are only understood as we serve a particular people in a particular area. Imagine if someone from another faith trained in Christianity came to the United States to share his or her views with us. While that person may be able to gain an understanding of some core issues, should he study Catholicism, Protestantism, or the Orthodox tradition? Let's say he examines Protestantism. Should he then focus on the Baptist tradition, Presbyterianism, Pentecostalism, Methodism, the Moravians, Disciples of Christ, Nazarenes, or Lutherans? Recognizing the global numbers provides the scope of the pressure point, but understanding the peoples is key to reaching their hearts.

Questions to Consider

1. Have you encountered the views of pluralism and inclusivism? Can you describe how those perspectives were communicated? Were they held by those within the church or outside of the church?

2. Do you agree or disagree that pluralistic and inclusivistic views hinder the advancement of the good news that Jesus provides salvation to those who repent and place their faith in Him? Why?

3. How do you think the growth of Islam, particularly in the West, will influence society at large? How do you think it will practically affect gospel advancement across the world?

4. How do you think the growth of the "Nones," particularly in the West, will influence society at large? How do you think their number will affect gospel advancement across the world?

5. What practical steps do you and your church need to take to better understand the people living around you beyond the fact that your area may contain a large number of Muslims, Christians, Mormons, or Hindus?

5

International Migration

And he made from one man every nation
of mankind to live on all the face of the earth,
having determined allotted periods and the
boundaries of their dwelling place.

—ACTS 17:26

The Chos immigrated to Baltimore, Maryland. While there, they encountered a Nepali server in a restaurant. Over time they had the privilege of introducing her, and soon thereafter her family in the city, to Jesus. A church was then planted with these new believers. Members of the church then recognized they had relatives in Nepal and India who also needed to hear of the hope of Christ. So traveling along the social networks between the church members in Baltimore and those in Asia, two mission trips were organized. The immediate result was that several hundred people came to Jesus and churches were planted as a result of the gospel traveling across these international relationship lines.[1]

The church presently lives in what has been called the "Age of Migration."[2] At the moment, 3 percent of the world's peoples (about 214 million) reside outside of their countries of birth. If such a population represented a country, it would be the fifth largest nation on the planet. While much migration occurs within the Majority World countries, many of the world's peoples are moving to Western countries and represent some of the world's unreached and least reached peoples.

International migration is creating a pressure point that is providing the church with opportunities for gospel advancement unknown by previous generations.

History: The Story of Movement

The history of the peoples of the world is a history of migration. In the beginning, the command was given to Adam and Eve to "fill the earth" (Gen. 1:28). Their descendants multiplied, moved across the planet, and subdued it. Throughout the Old Testament we read of the movement of the peoples as a result of both obedience and disobedience to God, war, famine, slave trade, and political changes. In fact the history of mankind is a history of peoples on the move. Because space limits a detailed discussion of history, I will make a few summary statements regarding such movements and the West.

Shortly after the European explorers traveled to the New World, there was a significant increase in the number of peoples who immigrated (voluntarily or by force) to the areas of North and South America. Over the course of four hundred years, the Atlantic slave trade shipped thirteen million Africans to new lands. From 1800 to 1914, fifty million people settled in areas of Argentina, Australia, New Zealand, Canada, and the United States. At the beginning of this period, 4 percent of ethnic Europeans were living outside of their countries of birth; by the end the proportion had swelled to 21 percent.[3]

During the Industrial Era from 1850 to 1945, over thirty-five million Europeans departed for North America. Two million Scandinavians arrived in the New World. Four and a half million Irish arrived. Five million Italians immigrated. Over four million came from Great Britain. The area that would become the German Empire lost six million people. Three million emigrated from the Balkans and Asia Minor. And eight million Poles, Jews, Hungarians, Bohemians, Slovaks, Ukrainians, and Ruthenians navigated the Atlantic to live in the Western world.[4] From the 1880s to the 1930s, France also received a large number of immigrants, with over two million coming from Spain, Italy, Belgium, and Poland.[5]

Changes in US and Canadian immigration policies in the 1960s helped facilitate a geographical shift in the nations represented by those arriving in these countries. Until this time, waves of Europeans dominated the migrant landscape. However, since the latter part of the twentieth century, there have been large increases of immigrants coming from Latin America, Asia, and Africa. Advancements in telecommunications and air travel, ethnic cleansing, the collapse of the Soviet Empire, wars, and famine all contributed to the rise in the number of peoples who have migrated since the latter half of the twentieth century.

The Divine Maestro

Do you hear the movement being played on the instruments of the nations as orchestrated by the Divine Maestro? Listen. It's playing next door. In his address on Mars Hill, Paul was attempting to share the gospel with the Athenians. In the middle of his address, he made a brief but very important statement related to the sovereign will of God and the nations: "And he made from one man every nation of mankind to live on all the face of the earth, having determined allotted periods and the boundaries of their dwelling place, that they should seek God, and perhaps feel their way toward him and find him. Yet he is actually not far from each one of us" (Acts 17:26–27). What is clear from this passage is that the Creator is sovereign over His creation. All the nations of the world have a bloodline running back to Adam and Eve. God is Lord over the history and habitations of His people. The practical reality of these theological truths reveals the outworking of His salvation history among the peoples of the world as they migrate across the planet in search of a home. The book of Revelation reveals the fulfillment of His work as the faces of the nations are observed around the throne (Rev. 7:9).

From a sociological perspective, there are various push-pull factors in play as to why people migrate. Push factors move people out of their homelands. These are often negative and may include war, famine, persecution, poverty, and disasters. Pull factors draw people to other locations. Generally, these are more positive matters such as the hope for a better way of life, material wealth, better education, safety, and freedom. While these factors operate throughout the world, the reality is that a Divine Maestro is working through the good, bad, and ugly so that the nations of the world may find Him.

- Between 1990 and 2010, the more developed countries gained 45 million international immigrants, an increase of 55 percent.

- Between 1990 and 2010, the migrant population of the less developed countries increased by 13 million (18 percent).

- Between 2000 and 2010, nine countries gained over one million international migrants: United States (8 million), Spain (4.6 million), Italy (2.3 million), Saudi Arabia (2.2 million), United Kingdom (1.7 million), Canada (1.6 million), Syria (1.3 million), Jordan (1 million), and United Arab Emirates (1 million).[6]

- By 2010, immigrants comprised 22 percent of the population of Australia, 21.3 percent of Canada, 13.5 percent of the United States, and 10.4 percent of the United Kingdom.[7]

- The main nationalities granted British citizenship in 2008 were Indian (11,285), Pakistani (9,440), Iraqi (8,895), Somali (7,165), and Zimbabwean (5,710).[8]
- By 2017, one Canadian in five could be a visible minority race.[9]

While it is easy to get lost in the numbers from across the globe, we must remember that each one represents someone created in the image of God in need of salvation or to serve on mission with Him. In light of the work of the Divine Maestro, the church must ask how she should respond in the age of migration. This pressure point creates many challenges and opportunities. Not only has the Lord told us to go into the entire world, but He is also bringing the world to our neighborhoods. Some of these represent the world's unreached people groups. Reaching them with the gospel and partnering with them to carry this good news along their social networks across the globe is an opportunity for mission that the church must recognize and seize.

God Is Working in the United States

This book is on global pressure points, and international migration makes global issues relevant in the United States in particular. The United States is the world's largest immigrant-receiving nation and has been for many years. We receive approximately 20 percent of the world's migrating population. No other nation comes anywhere close to this percentage.

Countries with the Highest Numbers of International Migrants, 2010.[10]

Country	Estimated number of international immigrants at mid-year, 2010	As Percentage of Global Total
United States	42,813,281	20
Russian Federation	12,270,388	5.7
Germany	10,758,061	5
Saudi Arabia	7,288,900	3.4
Canada	7,202,340	3.4
France	6,684,842	3.1
United Kingdom	6,451,711	3
Spain	6,377,524	3
India	5,436,012	2.5
Ukraine	5,257,527	2.5

Here is a quick glimpse of some of the present realities of this pressure point:

- It is estimated that there are 361 unreached people groups in the United States.[11]
- For the first time in US history, births to minorities are now the majority.[12]
- By 2043, the United States is expected to become a minority-majority nation, with the non-Hispanic white population no longer the majority.[13]
- The states with the highest percentage of foreign born in their populations are California (27 percent), New York (22 percent), and New Jersey (21 percent).
- New York, Texas, and Florida accounted for 30 percent of the foreign-born population. Including California, these four states are home to more than half of all foreign born.
- Half of the foreign born are between the ages of eighteen and forty-four, compared with about one-third of the native born.

- Over one-third of the foreign-born population came in 2000 or later.

- About 85 percent of the foreign-born population speak a language other than English at home, compared with about 10 percent of the native population.

- One in ten foreign born do not speak English at all.[14]

Students

Soon after I arrived in Birmingham, I had the privilege of meeting Yoshua, who is a member of our church. Yoshua came to the United States from Nicaragua to study at a university here. During his studies, a fellow classmate befriended him and eventually invited him to a worship gathering. After attending twice, Yoshua placed his faith in Christ and began to grow in his new life. Though he came from a Catholic background, he had very little knowledge of the Bible. He soon found himself regularly studying God's Word and serving others. Shortly thereafter, he sensed the Spirit leading him into pastoral ministry. When I met him, he was helping provide leadership to a Hispanic congregation that was started from our faith family. I recently heard Yoshua share his story of how the Lord orchestrated his move to Birmingham to bring him to faith. While studying in the states, Yoshua said that he very clearly sensed the Lord wanting him to return to Nicaragua to serve as a pastor and be involved in training other pastors and missionaries who will plant churches.

Each year students leave their countries of birth to study abroad. The West is still the primary destination for many students, with the United States boasting 764,000 such students during the 2011–2012 academic year, a record high. Much of this growth comes from the increased number of Chinese and Saudi Arabian students. At the time of this writing, the University of Southern California, the University of Illinois at Urbana-Champaign, New York University, Purdue University, and Columbia University have the highest numbers of international students in the United States. The following table provides a glimpse at the numbers of students coming to the United States from some of the least reached contexts in the world.

Select Places of Origin of International Students in US, 2011–2012[15]

Country	2011–12 Academic Year
China	194,000
India	100,000
South Korea	72,000
Saudi Arabia	34,000
Taiwan	23,000
Japan	20,000
Vietnam	15,500
Turkey	12,000
Nepal	9,600
Hong Kong	8,000
Thailand	7,600
Indonesia	7,100
Nigeria	7,000
Iran	7,000
Malaysia	6,700

Of course, the United States is not the only Western location for such students. England is no stranger to the strangers from across the world. Take Sheffield, for example. Here is a city with students from many different countries, including China, Malaysia, India, Cyprus, Nigeria, Sri Lanka, Saudi Arabia, Pakistan, Libya, and Taiwan. Across the English Channel, France welcomes students from across the world. During the 2011–2012 academic year, Morocco, China, Algeria, Tunisia, Senegal, Germany, Italy, Cameroon, Vietnam, and Spain were the top ten locations for international students studying in France.[16] Consider the following table showing some of the numbers of international students studying in Australia.

Places of Origin of International Students in Australia, 2011 Secondary and Non-secondary School Enrollments[17]

Country	Enrollments of secondary and non-secondary school in 2011
China	160,000
India	73,000
Republic of Korea	30,000
Vietnam	24,000
Malaysia	23,000
Thailand	22,000
Indonesia	18,000
Nepal	18,000
Brazil	15,000
Saudi Arabia	12,000

Throughout history, the Spirit has often worked in powerful ways among student populations to bring about awakenings and great missionary movements. Could the Divine Maestro be bringing the nations to the West where the gospel is prevalent that He may birth a movement among some of the unreached and unengaged as those students return home?

Refugees

As I write this portion of this chapter, it is only a few days before Christmas, and while many of us will have the delight of taking time to remember the birth of the Prince of Peace, others are fleeing for their lives. Just before writing this section, I checked the headlines for matters related to refugees and encountered news such as a call for hygiene items for Syrian refugees fleeing into

Turkey. It is estimated that during this month 230,000
Syrians will have fled their homeland due to violence.[18]
I quickly checked another newspaper to read of an organization in Austin, Texas, that is working to help settle
Burmese refugees in that city.[19] Another story from a
former Johannesburg reporter shares that three hundred thousand people fled to Zambia to escape the fight-
ing in the Democratic Republic of Congo.[20] Where there
is violence, persecution, and threats to life, refugees will
be on the move, often crossing borders.

While the plight of the refugee has been around for
centuries, the twentieth century could be considered the
age of the refugee.[21] Following World War II, the number
of people fleeing their countries of residence skyrocketed,
so the department of the United Nations High Commissioner for Refugees (UNHCR) was established. The original plan was for this department to exist for three years
with an annual budget of US$300,000 to assist with the
large number of displaced Europeans. Since that time,
however, the evils of the world and numbers of refugees
increased so dramatically that the office now oversees
34.4 million people and maintains a budget exceed-
ing US$2 billion.[22] The official definition of a refugee
embraced by the UNHCR is related to someone who has

> well-founded fear of being persecuted for reasons of race,
> religion, nationality, membership of a particular social
> group or political opinion, is outside the country of his
> nationality and is unable or, owing to such fear, is
> unwilling to avail himself of the protection of that coun-
> try; or who, not having a nationality and being outside
> the country of his former habitual residence as a result
> of such events, is unable or, owing to such fear, is unwill-
> ing to return to it.[23]

There are two other closely related categories that
have developed in the age of the refugee. An *asylum
seeker* is someone who has made application to a country

for refugee status whose case has not yet been processed. Someone is considered *internally displaced* if he remains in his country but is separated from his home.

Of all of the international migrants, refugees are among those in the direst situations. The refugees of the world swim in a sea of uncertainty and crisis. Often they will flee their homelands, only to find themselves living in nearby refugee camps sometimes for years before being relocated to another country. Once in this new land, the cultures, language, and people are very strange. Consider the many Somali refugees who have been settled in Louisville, Kentucky. Imagine the culture shock of the Somali when it comes to learning how to shop, pay bills, mail letters, enroll children in school, and understand one of the world's most difficult languages while in a world that is far from the conservative morality of African Muslim life.

The opportunities to serve refugees are numerous. They need assistance in learning language and culture. They simply need a friend as they attempt to stay afloat. The church has much hope to share with those who often feel hopeless. Consider that by the end of 2011, there were 42.5 million forcibly displaced persons living in the world. Of those

- 4.3 million people were newly displaced due to conflict or persecution.
- 25.9 million were comprised of 10.4 million refugees and 15.5 million internally displaced persons connected to the UNHCR, which was 700,000 more people than in 2010.
- 12 million were stateless.
- Four-fifths of the world's refugees were hosted by developing countries.
- Pakistan was host to the largest number of refugees (1.7 million), followed by Iran (887,000) and Syria (755,400).

- Afghanistan was the leading country of origin for refugees.
- 532,000 refugees were repatriated voluntarily.
- The United States received 51,500 refugees.
- More than 876,100 people submitted applications for asylum or refugee status. South Africa received the most applications, followed by the United States and France.
- 17,700 asylum applications were submitted in 69 countries by unaccompanied or separated children, mostly Afghani and Somali.
- 48 percent of refugees and 50 percent of all internally displaced persons and returnees (former refugees) were women and girls.
- Children comprised 46 percent of refugees and 34 percent of asylum-seekers.[24]

The Potential of the Strangers Next Door

The call to reach the nations that have migrated to our neighborhoods is not a call to neglect to send missionaries to Majority World countries where large numbers of unreached peoples exist. We have been told to go and must continue to do so, for the greatest needs for the gospel and church multiplication exist in the non-Western world. However, something is missionally malignant whenever we are willing to make great sacrifices to travel the world to reach a people group but are not willing to walk across the street. The church is foolish to think that it pleases the Lord when we travel to another country to reach a people when representatives of that people group fly past us over the Pacific and land in our airports to settle in our communities, but we make no effort to reach them. In view of this pressure point, the churches and mission agencies that are likely to thrive in the realm of missions are those who integrate their domestic and international strategies and stop operating from the long-standing model that consisted of silos separating the "domestic" and "foreign."

With the peoples of the world on the move, there are numerous opportunities for kingdom advancement. Recognizing the importance of international migration, in 2010 a group of missiologists developed a booklet to raise awareness on this matter. *Scattered to Gather: Embracing the Global Trend of Disaspora* outlines three helpful ways of thinking about missions and migration.[25]

Missions to the Diasporas

This understanding is the notion of making disciples of those peoples on the move who do not know the Lord. With numerous peoples moving for work, study, or better quality of life or fleeing persecution, disaster, war, or famine, there are many opportunities to share the gospel with those who do not know Him. When I wrote *Strangers Next Door: Immigration, Migration and Mission*, drawing attention to the large numbers of unreached people groups migrating to the Western world, missions to the diasporas was what I had in mind.[26]

Missions Through the Diasporas

This concept explains the disciple-making work of those who have migrated and are working to reach their own people group living with them in their new homelands. I once had a Korean student tell me that whenever the Chinese migrate they begin a restaurant in their new country, whenever the Japanese migrate they begin a business, but whenever the Koreans migrate they plant Korean churches! There is much truth to this student's humor. I have also worked with Haitians, Nepali, and West Africans who have planted churches among their peoples who also migrated to the States. In

some countries recent immigrants are catching a vision
to plant churches among their fellow countrymen who
have also recently migrated. Oftentimes the arrival into
a new context where religious freedom is widespread
creates an openness to the gospel.

Missions Beyond the Diasporas

Many peoples leave home for better employment in
the Middle East, South America, or Asia, and they go
with a vision of crossing cultures to make disciples and
multiply churches. For those who do not, such a vision for
the nations needs to be put before them. International
migrants reaching other peoples is known as missions
beyond the diasporas. For example, this expression is
observed whenever Chinese brothers and sisters living
in diaspora are sharing the gospel with Somalis or when
Brazilians are planting churches in the Muslim world
among Iraqis.

Thousands of Filipinos are employed throughout
Hong Kong as domestic workers. Marietta—a follower
of Jesus—migrated from the Philippines and works as a
nanny for a Chinese family there. One day she attended
a training event designed to equip strategically posi-
tioned nannies to make disciples. The training also
involved distributing the *Jesus* film. One stormy morning school was delayed for the children, so they had to
remain home with Marietta. Knowing that Jesus calmed
a storm, she showed the children the clip of the film in
Cantonese portraying this event and asked the children
if they would like to ask Jesus to calm the storm over
their city that morning. By the afternoon, the storm
was gone and the children were able to attend class—
now with an understanding that Jesus calms storms.
Following this, Marietta was provided an opportunity
to share the gospel with the parents. Her employers are
now followers of Jesus and active members of a local
congregation in Hong Kong.[27]

The movement of the nations of the world is a very complex matter. It not only has a long history, but also many implications on the mission of the church. While the peoples of the earth migrate for a variety of reasons, the sovereign Lord is behind such movements as a part of the outworking of His story of redemption and restoration of all things. The nations of the world live among us. Will we respond appropriately to this pressure point of our day?

Questions to Consider

1. How can you best communicate to your church the global realities of the peoples on the move?

2. What challenges and opportunities does this pressure point pose for your church?

3. Who are the unreached people groups living in your area? What are their countries of birth? How did they get to your neighborhood? Are there any churches reaching out to them?

4. What are some practical ways that you can reach out to the foreign-born, including students and refugees, living in your area? How will you connect with them, serve them, share the gospel, teach them obedience, equip them, and partner with them to reach their people group and others?

CHAPTER

6

Globalization

It's a small, small world.

—RICHARD M. SHERMAN
AND ROBERT B. SHERMAN[1]

Near Cape Spear, the easternmost point of continental North America, is St. John's Newfoundland. From here you can be one of the first to observe the sunrise from North America. Overlooking St. John's is a historical site known as Signal Hill. I have stood there on different occasions glancing across the North Atlantic. It was here in 1901 that Guglielmo Marconi received the first transatlantic wireless signal. What once took an enormous amount of planning and cost to send and receive a tiny message from Europe now happens multitudes of times every second, covering much greater distances with enormous amounts of information at an inexpensive rate.

We live in the instant. Human interconnectedness has increased across the globe. On my phone, I can get news of protest marches happening in Cairo, Skype with someone in Tokyo, and receive e-mails from Bangladesh—simultaneously. We move in the moment. A person can physically be anywhere on the planet within forty-eight hours. Safer and more efficient air travel, better road systems, and automobiles, trains, and boats have shortened the distances between the peoples of the world. Globalization has resulted in an accelerated, compressed, and intensive way of life for many. All areas of life including economics, religion, family dynamics, and education have been affected by this pressure point. In fact, globalization is intertwined with many of the other pressure points found in the book.

It's a Small World

My children enjoy taking a family trip to Orlando, Florida. Of course, we visit the Magic Kingdom at Walt Disney World. We also have to ride It's a Small World—multiple times. My own socio-anthropological tendencies need to be satisfied for the day, and my kids love it.

While I doubt Walt Disney was being intentionally prophetic in predicting the "shrinking" of the world brought about by globalization, inexpensive and rapid international travel, global commerce, and advancements in telecommunications when he created this ride, the reality is that the world is smaller today—metaphorically speaking—than when the ride was developed decades ago.

For example, the other day I was looking at an orange, a banana, and a lemon in my kitchen. The labels on each item revealed a different country of origin. Today I am able to have such international representatives in my house with little thought given to such a matter. In fact, if I run out of such fruit, I can jump in my Japanese car—built in the United States—be at the grocery store in a matter of minutes, and get my fruit from three other countries of the world. And not give it a second thought.

When my grandparents were my age, such was not a possibility. When my parents were my age, they may have been able to have a similar experience. So while the expression, "It's a small world," is now a cliché, it is true. Neither my grandparents (Builders) nor my parents (Baby Boomers) experienced young adulthood with instant communication and such rapid transportation.

While the forces of globalization have been in motion for centuries, their influence on the world has exponentially increased in the last few decades.

The Blowing Winds of Change

The world experienced significant changes during the industrial revolution and with the fall of Communism in the latter twentieth century. The forces of globalization have existed as people have moved, interacted, and sought better ways of life, and the rise of the capitalist system and modernity catalyzed social and technological progress. For example, centuries of social connections between nations, corporations, and individuals and scientific and mathematical developments had to occur before I could have a laptop computer on which I am writing this chapter. Keyboards had to be developed that followed electric and manual typewriters. Going further back in time, even the English language had to develop from other languages and alphabets.

Starting with the early modern period of the sixteenth century and concluding with modernity of the latter twentieth century, seismic shifts occurred. Centuries of social and technological pressures had built until they facilitated substantial changes in global cultures. It was during this time that European colonialism occurred. The British, French, and Spanish began to obtain territories across the world. New trade routes were established, aided by nautical advancements that themselves were shaped by astronomical developments such as the astrolabe and the sextant. It should also be noted that advancements from the Islamic and Chinese societies influenced and aided European developments. The growth of cities, movement of millions of African slaves to the Americas, and growth of capitalism resulted in the movement of ideas, technology, and cultures from one society to another. Political developments between nation-states, rise of global banking systems, steam-powered locomotives, telegraphs, radios, telephones, and numerous other scientific advancements unfolded during this time. There were agricultural advancements, medical advancements, and population growth. Large numbers of people began emigrating for the New World, and European colonialism began to decline. Following both world wars, numerous changes occurred between nations affecting trade, communication, and development. The automobile and commercial airlines made travel more efficient. And with such mobility came the rapid exchange of ideas, products, and services.

With the development of the Internet, the ubiquitous use of cell phones (and smartphones), and the large waves of migration happening across the world, the exchange of ideas, cultures, and goods and services now happens at an unprecedented rate. Online shopping and overnight shipping have made a 24/7 business model the expectation. The movement of large sums of money can now happen at the click of a mouse. Major business decisions are made without the involved parties being physically present in the same room. A corporate decision in a high-rise boardroom in Japan can greatly affect the livelihood of the future grandchildren of a factory worker living in rural Indiana. When the winds of change blow in the world today, the entire world feels it.

When I was a child, I sometimes dismantled my battery-operated toys to see how they worked. What appeared as a truck in the store's package was actually composed of several interconnected parts. Leave one part out of the toy and the truck would not function properly. Globalization is a complex process comprised of several parts that are often integrated and interdependent. Manfred B. Steger notes that "globalization is not a single process but a set of processes that operate simultaneously and unevenly on several levels and in various dimensions."[2] He points out that it cannot be reduced to one dimension and has effects in the realms of economics, politics, cultures, ecologies, and ideologies.

From Solids to Liquids

Globalization can be described as a shrinking effect, whereby the social connections of people and organizations continue to become more and more tightly connected. In his book *Globalization: The Essentials*, George Ritzer uses a set of metaphors to understand the complexity of globalization.[3] The first pair of metaphors describe globalization in terms of solidity and liquidity. Before the present age of globalization, matters related to people, information, and locations were solid and tended to be rigid. As a result of this hardness, people did not travel often, and ideas were slow to transfer from place to place. While many examples of the world being a solid place exist, this period of time could be identified with the Cold War and the fall of communism. The nation-state and its desire to control and maintain were examples of a solid world.

Today's world seems to have moved from a state of solidity to that of fluidity. The mobility of people and the exchange of ideas now happen at a rapid rate. The solid structures of yesterday appear to be melting. Food, automobiles, and clothes are now transferred from country to country. Both legal and illegal items now travel quickly across what appears to be a borderless world. The barriers erected by the nation-states have become more porous over time, allowing for the liquid of people, ideas, and products to move more freely without governmental control.

The church needs to be aware of the blessings of innovation and technology that have been moving the world in a direction of liquidity. Great opportunities for global disciple making often arise as advancements come onto the scene of human history. For example, the missionary activities of the apostolic and early church were aided by the Roman road system of their days. Consider the great help of the steam-powered locomotive to the kingdom. What about the automobile? Yes, these advancements made travel safer, faster, and more efficient. But was that the extent of their value? Were they allowed to develop simply so we could get to grandmother's house in time for Christmas? They are wonderful blessings, but is there a bigger picture?

I read an article in the *Telegraph* that caused me to stop and consider how economic improvement across Asia is likely to lead to greater opportunities for the gospel to spread rapidly and with honor (2 Thess. 3:1). As China and India continue to support a growing middle class, the demand for air travel increases. And with demand comes the need for more pilots. The article went on to note that Asian airlines were going to have to recruit Western pilots because there were not enough Asian pilots to meet the demand of the customers.[4]

The growth in the demand for people to take advantage of the technology of flight is so great that William Voss, president of Flight Safety Foundation, was quoted in the article as stating, "Never in human history have we seen a time when two billion people will enter the middle class and demand air travel. That time is now."[5] The number of Asians traveling within their countries and across the globe is likely to grow dramatically in the next several years. The church needs to recognize the opportunity for gospel advancement in this rise of the Asian middle class. For every new Asian pilot who enters the workforce, opportunities greatly increase for unreached peoples living in Asia to come in contact with the gospel as they travel the world and encounter followers of Jesus. Also, the increasing flights into and within Asia allow more and more opportunities for followers of Jesus to travel and spread this good news. The movement from "solids" to "liquids" is an opportunity to increase exponentially the dissemination of the message of hope to the nations.

From Heavy to Light

The second pair of metaphors Ritzer used to explain globalization is that of the world moving from being heavy to light. Industrial and preindustrial societies were characterized as heavy. People remained in a location to farm land; they were difficult to move. The shipping of material goods often involved the movement of heavy objects at a slow pace and with much expense. Early books were often printed on heavy paper. The first computers were large enough to fill a room. Phone booths took up sidewalk space and contained large books known as telephone directories. A letter had to be written on paper, sealed in an addressed envelope, and stamped with the appropriate amount of postage before it would be carried via automobile to its destination, some time later.

As technology advanced, items became lighter and easier to transport from location to location. Weightless books can now exist in electronic form. Cellular phones now fit in one's pocket. Transcontinental and international travel takes hours by plane, as opposed to weeks by wagon or boat. Messages now travel to the farthest reaches of the globe in seconds and with little expense. VHS has been replaced with DVDs, which are now giving way to streaming movies.

Problems of Globalization

Not everything about globalization is positive. Though the church does not have control over the contextual issues that apply pressure to her, she is able to leverage many such pressures for kingdom advancement. However, while we have to live and move on mission in light of globalization, we must realize that globalization has brought with it many problems. Multinational corporations and other big business have often done much harm in one part of the world in order to reap the benefits of globalization in another part of the world. It has been argued that the rich get richer and the poor get poorer. Some companies have taken advantage of Majority World nations in order to make money. Destruction of habitats and environmental pollution have been the fallout from some companies seeking to take advantage of business in a world that is more "liquid" and "light."

The rapid movement of people has also allowed diseases to spread faster. A tightly connected world is one in which a pandemic could quickly become a reality, with the ill being too numerous to quarantine. Such movement of the nations has also continued to facilitate human trafficking, sale of illegal drugs, and rapid dissemination of pornography. Terrorists also benefit from globalization. Even Osama bin Laden took advantage of advancements in telecommunications, transportation, and weapons for his evil deeds.

Practices Under Pressure

While globalization is a force of change, the church must recognize that she is not to conform to any ungodliness that is found with this pressure. Rather, she is called to remain faithful in a rapidly changing, tightly connected, flat world. The following are just a few practices for consideration in light of this pressure point.

Delight in Grace

While the blessings of God abound, He has particularly provided grace in the area of connections. Gone are the days when missionaries set sail for another land while giving up regular connections with loved ones back home. Communication would be delayed by months, and return trips were few if ever. Now we have the blessings of instant verbal, textual, and visual communications with loved ones back home. Return trips are quick and practical. Globalization has allowed interpersonal connections to remain both regular and strong.

Practice Strategic Integration

Missionary strategies for "over here" must be developed in light of our missionary strategies for "over there." For centuries we have treated domestic missions and international missions as two strangers on two different paths that should never cross. While there remain significant distinctions between near-culture evangelism and distant-culture evangelism, global shifts are causing some to reconsider the unhealthy dichotomy of "home" and "foreign" missions. The church needs to reconsider the idea that the world is her parish. Better communication and planning are necessary among kingdom citizens scattered across the nations. Better communication and planning are necessary among church leaders overseeing local church missionary activity. Better communication and planning are necessary among mission agencies.

Develop Majority World Partnerships

If denominations and churches should be integrating their strategies for global disciple making, then they should develop partnerships with local churches in other nations. While I recognize this has been taking place among some kingdom citizens and that there are numerous challenges to such partnerships, wise stewardship under this pressure point will develop healthy relationships between churches in the West and those in Majority World nations.

Those of us in the West will feel the tension between paternalism and an abdication of our responsibilities. We must not repeat the problems of the past; however, we must not discard the wisdom and experience the Father has provided us. Do we have much to learn from our brothers and sisters? Yes. But do we have much to contribute as well? Yes.

Labor Among the Diasporas

More than two hundred million people are presently living outside of their countries of birth. Many of these peoples are followers of Jesus, and many are not. We need to consider how best to minister to, through, and beyond the diasporas (see chapter 5). Some are kingdom servants in need of equipping and encouragement, potential powerhouses for the multiplication of disciples, leaders, and churches. Others have traveled land, air, and sea and are in need of the good news for themselves and their people. We live in an age of migration, a time of such mass movements unlike any other in history. It would be wise for us to reflect deeply on Acts 17:26–27 as we recognize the kingdom opportunities now present among the peoples on the move.

Leverage Technology

Globalization has helped foster incredible advancements in communications. Consider the influence of YouTube, Facebook, and Twitter over the past few years, especially in North Africa. These developments have facilitated globalization. Travel to some of the poorest areas in the world, and you are guaranteed to find people with cellular phones. They may have little food and clothes, but phones will be in their hands. While the computer is still very important to globalization, the mobile phone is becoming even more influential. For example, by the end of 2011 mobile-cellular subscriptions reached six billion. The global population is seven billion. From 2010 to 2011, subscriptions increased by more than six hundred million, with almost all of them coming from the developing world. China has one billion subscribers. It was predicted that India would reach one billion subscribers in 2012. The growth of smartphones and tablets are leading the way and making a significant contribution. By the end of 2011, 2.3 billion people were using the Internet. This is more than one-third of the world's population.[6]

Such advances in communications can be used for evangelism, equipping, and leadership development. I had a student tell me of his brief trip to China in which a girl came to faith through the witness of his team. By the time he and the team returned to the United States, he was informed by the girl that she had introduced some friends living on the opposite side of the country to Christ via texting. Several years ago, Canadian National Baptist Convention leaders needed a way to train pastors in their denomination. Because Canada is a very large land mass (second largest in the world behind Russia), their pastors lived too far from one another for frequent face-to-face training. As a result they started videoing much of their training and putting it online. Such use of videos has become commonplace.

A new believer in China. A denomination in Canada. They saw the possibilities and leveraged them for the kingdom.

Business as Mission

The method of legitimate for-profit companies being started across the world, while simultaneously providing opportunities for disciple making and church multiplication, is becoming more and more common. Also, the importance of the tentmaker—one who is completely supported through marketplace ministry—is likely to continue to grow in the days to come. Since globalization has opened many markets across the world, followers of Jesus need to consider how to best position themselves in the global marketplace. There is a great need for church-planting teams to work among the nations as they labor in the marketplace each day. The kingdom

ethic, rather than the ethic of capitalism, is to take priority over any ungodly business practices. Priorities must
be in order. Miriam Adeney has reminded us, "Making
cross-cultural connections has been our mandate from
the beginning. Our involvement in globalization is not
in economics but in God's love for his world."[7]

Prepare for Possible Backlash

Globalization has often been equated with the West
in general and the United States in particular. Right or
wrong, such is the reality, and pressure comes with it.
In certain parts of the world, there is not only a growing anti-Western sentiment but a growing anti-United
States sentiment. Often such environments are found
in the countries where many unreached peoples reside.

It is likely in the days to come that such negative feelings will continue to grow. While the blessings of globalization are with us, so are the consequences of unethical
and ungodly ways connected with this pressure point.
It should not come as a surprise if we find ourselves
being opposed not only for the sake of the gospel but
also because we are from a Western country, particularly the United States. The day may come when our
nationality hinders global disciple making. We need to
recognize this possible future and labor while we can as
we still have opportunity.

Also, we need to continue to equip Majority World
church leaders to make disciples and multiply churches.
And we need to train them in such a way that once they
are equipped, they are not dependent on us.

* * *

One of the games that I used to play and have played
with my children is Pick-up Sticks. The game consists of
a pile of overlapping, differently colored, small sticks not
much thicker than a toothpick. The object is to remove
the more valuable sticks without bumping or moving

any of the other sticks in the pile. It takes a very steady hand and much patience. The movement of any given stick, because it is resting on a multitude of other sticks, is likely to set off a chain reaction of movement, thus ending the player's turn.

The influence of globalization has created a world of pick-up sticks. What happens in one context often influences another context in the world. While globalization has helped facilitate increases in ungodliness, the interconnected world in which we now live has incredible opportunities for global disciple making, unlike those known to any previous generation.

We live in a flat world, one where the distant is near and the exotic is familiar. Unless present global infrastructures disintegrate, it is likely that the world will continue to shrink in the days to come. Technological, economic, and travel advancements will accelerate the pulling together of the continents into a virtual and practical Pangaea. Widespread contextual shifts demand that the church make wise adjustments to her missionary strategy in making disciples of all nations. While the truth of the never-changing gospel that was once for all delivered to the saints remains (Jude 3), wise stewardship involves methodological adjustment with the ever-changing contexts.

Questions to Consider

1. How have you and your church benefited from globalization? Has globalization impacted you in a negative way? If so, how?

2. What are some of the practices mentioned above that your church could use to make disciples of all nations?

3. Can you think of additional practices not mentioned in this chapter that the church should consider in light of this pressure point? What are they?

CHAPTER

7

Poverty

Remember the poor.

—GALATIANS 2:10

Shortly after moving to Birmingham, I had the privilege of meeting Ben, one of the church planters sent out from The Church at Brook Hills. Ben and I had lunch together in the community in which he lives. As I drove to the restaurant, the homes became older in appearance and more run down. The deeper I traveled into the neighborhood, more and more businesses had bars on their windows. This was not the neighborhood of most church planters today.

At a time when many people are attempting to move out of the most dangerous and impoverished area of our city, Ben and several families from our church moved in to serve the poor and share the gospel with them. Giving up middle-class comforts and security, these families live among the poor and journey with them each day. Their church provides a cup of water and bread for the stomach, but it primarily offers living water and the bread of life.

Poverty is not new. It is a pressure point that remains. Will the church—especially in the West—run from it or, like Ben and the church-planting families, run to it?

As Old as the Garden

Poverty manifests itself in different expressions. The most obvious is *material poverty*: a lack of food, clothing, or shelter necessary to sustain healthy life. Less obvious is *relational poverty*: the lack of healthy social networks that serve as both a means of relational connection with others as well as a support system for survival in any given social context. People lacking material wealth but having the right support system are often able to move beyond their poverty. *Spiritual poverty* manifests in communities that lack a biblical expression of intimacy with the Creator and Sustainer of life.

Poverty, in all of its manifestations, is nothing new. It existed one thousand years ago. It existed two thousand years ago. It has existed for millennia. However, such was not always the case.

Returning to the Garden, we discover that poverty was nonexistent. In their pre-fallen state, Adam and Eve had all they needed for healthy life. God had placed them where they were allowed to eat from all of the trees except one (Gen. 2:16–17). Knowing that man is a relational being and that isolation is not a good thing, Eve was created (Gen. 2:21–22). Spiritual poverty was not an issue, for they walked in intimacy with God, hearing His voice on a regular basis.

Following the entrance of sin into the world, the quest for provision began. Adam's work in the garden was no longer without struggle; now the ground would resist his efforts (Gen. 3:17–19). The closeness that this husband and wife had known for some time would be forever strained (Gen. 3:16), and the fellowship with God was now broken (Rom. 3:10–12). The need to clothe oneself was now a reality and a reminder of such separation. In spite of sin that would eventually manifest in a multitude of ways, including deep and systemic poverty compounded over the millennia, God offered a promise and hope (Gen. 3:15).

In the Old Testament we read that once the Israelites settled in the Promised Land, the Lord instructed them to care for the poor because they would always be present (Deut. 15:11; Matt. 26:11) in a post-fallen world.

The book of Ruth provides a glimpse of the outworking of some of God's instructions to His people, namely that they were not to harvest everything from the field. Some food was to be left behind intentionally for those in need (Lev. 23:22; Ruth 2:7).

The New Testament has numerous references to the poor. Jesus publicly announced the beginning of His ministry by referencing His work among the poor (Luke 4:18). Widows in the church are provided assistance with food (Acts 6:1). Offerings are collected for churches in need (Acts 11:27–30). Paul reminded his readers of his pleasure to assist the poor (Gal. 2:10). James reminded the diasporic believers not to show prejudice against the poor (James 2:1–7). Revelation concludes by drawing numerous images from the Old Testament and the Garden, reminding believers that a day is coming when celebration (Rev. 19:1–8) and the healing of the nations will occur (Rev. 22:1–3). Poverty, in all of its manifestations, will be no more.

Until that day arrives, the church continues to find herself on mission in a world where centuries of the effects of poverty have been compounded across generations. The material, social, and spiritual needs of the peoples of the world are great. The spiritual poverty among the unreached was addressed in chapter 1. This chapter will address the present manifestation of material poverty.

The Pressure in the World

Global poverty is often measured in cost per living per day. In 2008 the World Bank revised its standard poverty line from US$1 per day earnings to US$1.25, based on 2005 prices. Between 2000 and 2008, the percentage of people living below the poverty line (in every region of the developing world) declined. Yet during 2008, an estimated 1.29 billion people in the world were still living on no more than US$1.25 per day. That is 22 percent of the developing world.

Across the various regions of the world, the World Bank notes the following poverty rates (2008 data):

- East Asia and the Pacific, 14%
- South Asia, 36%
- Latin America and the Caribbean, 6.5%
- Middle East and North Africa, 2.7%
- Eastern Europe and Central Asia, 0.5%
- Sub-Saharan Africa, 47%[1]

Many of the world's major cities have massive populations living in slums. By 2050 the number of slum dwellers is expected to reach 2 billion people. Across the world 1.5 billion people do not have access to a latrine, which helps contribute to the death of 1.5 million children each year who are raised in areas without proper sanitation and safe drinking water.[2]

Global Undernourishment

Whenever food consumption fails to meet dietary requirements on a regular basis, undernourishment exists. While significant reductions in poverty and undernourishment have been occurring, millions are still plagued by these realities in our fallen world. Between 2010 and 2012, it was estimated that 870 million people could be categorized as undernourished. This number represents a poor state of nutrition for every one in eight people in the world today. More than 850 million people in this category reside in developing countries.

Global Undernourishment by Region, 2010–2012[3]

Region	Undernourished in Millions, 2010–2012
Developed Regions	16
Southern Asia	304
Sub-Saharan Africa	234
Eastern Asia	167
South-Eastern Asia	65
Latin America/Caribbean	49
Western Asia/Northern Africa	25
Caucasus/Central Asia	6
Oceania	1

Challenges and Opportunities

Poverty creates a context in which numerous problems arise. For example, multitudes of men and women across the globe enter into prostitution to provide food for themselves, support for their children, and money for college tuition. In other situations parents have been known to sell their children into prostitution in order to survive. Human trafficking (defined as the holding of a person, by another person, in compelled service) thrives in impoverished context, and has become a multibillion-dollar business. Poverty is often coupled with a lower level of education among the people. For example, one of the most impoverished areas of the United States is Appalachia, which is also one of the areas with the least education.

Many of us in the West are disconnected from poverty in general, or at least from much of the poverty found throughout the Majority World. Paul Borthwick made several excellent comments and raised some outstanding questions as he reflected on this "disconnectedness":

The rich-poor gap presents us with many challenges. How can Western missionaries be prepared to go to the

poorest, most hostile areas of the world when our lifestyle adjustment is so severe? Can a generation raised on
lattes costing three dollars per cup be effective in a world
where millions have no access to clean drinking water?
Can Westerners who routinely spend eight to twelve dollars to see a movie live effectively alongside the one billion abjectly poor people living on less than one dollar per
day? In our techno-driven world of Twitter, smartphones
and Facebook, how will Westerners respond to living in
places that are technologically underdeveloped? . . . We
will need to adapt to simpler lifestyles *before* we go, to
live with diminished material expectations in an effort
to increase incarnational effectiveness.[4]

The church has always existed among the impoverished. From the first century until today, the Lord has
worked in mighty ways through those who were without many material assets in this world. In fact, much to
the surprise of His followers, Jesus was quick to point
out that it is difficult for the wealthy to enter into the
kingdom of God (Matt. 19:24). And while the gospel did
transform the hearts and lives of the wealthy, James
offers another example of a situation whereby the poor
were likely to be present during the church's assembly
and should be treated without prejudice (James 2:1–7).

In their book, *When Helping Hurts*, Steve Corbett and
Brian Fikkert note that not all poverty is the same and
any assistance should alleviate poverty while building
up and empowering the poor. They note that depending
on the circumstances, the church should help by providing relief, rehabilitation, and development. Relief
is emergency aid to be provided during serious crises;
rehabilitation begins after the crisis and restores people and communities to the beneficial aspects of their
pre-crisis conditions; development moves the people to
be who God has created them to be as workers who support themselves and their families.[5]

The pressure of poverty, like the other pressures mentioned in this book, must not distract the church from

her mission of making disciples of all nations. Help the poor and needy as we go? Absolutely. But as the church sends apostolic teams to make disciples, such teams must not become distracted. We must serve the poor while we preach the good news. The apostle Paul was a church planter who also had a heart for the poor. On one occasion he and Barnabas were delivering an offering to the church in Jerusalem during a time of desperate need (Acts 11:27–30). Paul noted his compassion for the poor when he wrote to the Galatians about remembering them (Gal. 2:10).

While established churches can do much in their areas to minister to the poor, care must be taken so that no expressions of paternalism manifest themselves. A church must not embrace a superior attitude and see herself as the savior to the people. Missionaries (particularly those with a background of a much higher standard of living) must also work to avoid any elements of paternalism in their church-planting endeavors. Such is a sure way to hinder the new believers' growth in Christ and possible church multiplication. Two hundred years of Protestant missionary travels to the Majority World have revealed the problems that have come about whenever missionaries fail to contextualize their labors, especially among the poor.

Disciples can be made and healthy churches can be planted among the literate and the illiterate. They can be birthed and grow in a Christ-pleasing manner among the highly educated and among those with little formal education. Churches are able to come into existence and function as the body of Christ in both wealthy and impoverished areas. The gospel and church membership know no socioeconomic boundaries.

This is an important fact. Rather than attempting to teach the new believers of an impoverished context ways of functioning as the church according to structures, organization, and methods more akin to wealthier nations, we must work to couch everything in the cultures of the peoples. Such work is known as contextualization, and it is the means of faithfully preaching the gospel, teaching new believers, seeing churches birthed, and multiplying churches among the poor of the world.

In the twentieth century Donald McGavran, missionary to India, observed a phenomenon among an impoverished people who embraced the gospel message. McGavran noted that as lives were transformed by the kingdom ethic of Christ, men would stop spending their money on alcoholic beverages and would use it for food and clothes. Rather than being slothful on the job, they would recognize that even their workday was to be unto the Lord. Over time, as people began to mature in Christ, McGavran commented that an upward social mobility occurred. He described this pattern as "redemption and lift."[6]

While life in the kingdom is not about a prosperity gospel, it is about a gospel that transforms the entire person and society. Whenever the kingdom ethic guides the lifestyles of the people in a tribe, village, or city, social changes begin to occur. Sometimes such changes result in many improving in their qualities of life. Of course, such is not always the case when Christians remain a small minority, so we should not make it a litmus test for faithfulness among believers. Many faithful followers of Jesus have lived in very poor conditions for years. We also should never use this transformation potential as an excuse to not assist those in desperate physical need. The love of Christ moves us to action—with assistance in our hands and the gospel on our tongues.

Questions for Consideration

1. What are the similarities and the differences between poverty in a country such as the United States and that of Ethiopia?

2. What are some cautions that you and your church need to keep in mind when it comes to making disciples of all nations while working among impoverished people? What are some social issues that could arise and sidetrack the mission of the church?

3. How could you and your church free up some financial resources to help advance the gospel and plant churches in areas of great physical need?

8

Growth of the Cities

*If current projections are anything to
go by, virtually the whole of the world's
demographic growth over the next 30 years
will be concentrated in urban areas.*

—UN Human Settlements Programme[1]

The church exists in an urban world, with over 50 percent of the global population residing in the cities. By 2030, it is expected that all of the developing regions of the world will have a majority of their populations living in the cities. Few people are able to escape the influence of urbanization. While global urbanization is not accelerating, its force will be felt for decades to come as urban populations continue to increase. It knows no geographical boundaries and extends even to the rural areas. Cities will continue to be places of rapid change, great population density, and global influence.

Over the past two hundred years, many Protestant advances occurred mainly in the rural areas. The urban context will require the church to think and minister differently. The cities pose a great challenge to the task of making disciples of all nations.

Defining Urban

It is helpful to begin with some definitions related to the topic of this chapter. Urban sociologist J. John Palen has defined *urbanization* as the number of people in urban places. Urbanization also refers to the process of people moving to the cities and has to do with growth. Closely related to urbanization is the development of urban culture. Such social patterns and behaviors manifesting themselves among those living in the cities is *urbanism.*[2]

To understand the urban contexts of the world, one must realize different governments define *urban* differently. Some countries define *urban* in terms of population. In the United States, the government generally identifies an urban community as having at least twenty-five hundred people. The Canadian government generally defines urban as a community with at least one thousand people. Denmark defines urban by two hundred fifty people. In China, urban is considered at least three thousand, and cities are identified with at least a population of sixty thousand. In Uganda, an urban context is more than two thousand. Other countries define urban in terms of economics, particularly the percent of people in nonagricultural occupations. Some governments define their urban areas by discerning if an urban culture exists and others by the administrative function of the areas.[3] Countries such as Venezuela, Argentina, Australia, and Brazil have large percentages of their populations in the urban contexts. China is approaching a majority of its population living in the cities. India, even with its large population and cities, still has a long way to go before half of its population is urban. The following table lists a select number of countries in the world and their urban percentages.

Select Countries with Urban Percentage of Population[4]

Country	Percent Urban
Venezuela	93
Argentina	92
Australia	89
Brazil	87
France	85
South Korea	83
United States	82
Saudi Arabia	82
Canada	81
United Kingdom	80
Mexico	78
Spain	77
Russian Federation	73
Iran	71
Turkey	70
Ukraine	69
Japan	67
Iraq	66
Algeria	66
North Korea	60
Angola	59
Cameroon	58
Morocco	58
Nigeria	50
China	47
Sudan	40
Pakistan	36
India	30

A Brief History of Urbanization

The first account of a city in the Bible is early in the book of Genesis. After the murder of Abel and God's confrontation with Cain, it is noted that Cain went away from the Lord's presence and built a city named after his son Enoch (Gen. 4:17). Archeologists have unearthed many early cities in Israel, Turkey, Iraq, Iran, Pakistan, Egypt, China, South America, Mexico, and Guatemala. During the first century, cities were located in many places. As the vision for the city continued to develop, many cities formed in the Western world. Urban dwellers were located in Crete, Greece, Rome, London, Paris, and Lyon. We can read about numerous places the first missionaries visited, such as Corinth, Philippi, and Ephesus. Many medieval cities whose populations numbered in the tens of thousands include Brussels, Pisa, Florence, and Naples. By the eighteenth century, thousands were also living in Amsterdam, Lisbon, Madrid, Vienna, and other cities, which meant that more than 10 percent of the world's population then lived in cities. In a little more than two hundred years, the majority of the world would be urban dwellers.

John J. Macionis and Vincent N. Parrillo described the development of the city as "a most decisive event in human history."[5] It was a means for people to increase in knowledge, interdependence, security, and synergy and an attempt to find a better way of life. And while this journey to our now-urban world has often been driven by a people's quest for a life without God—thus following in the footsteps of Cain—the city has also been a manifestation of God's grace working through man's sinfulness. In the city technology has been developed to improve the quality of life. The city has assisted in educational systems to advance our understandings of science and medicine. The city has served as a refuge and the catalyst for the improvement of health care, nutrition, and the arts. God's goodness has often come from the cities of the world. What people often mean for evil, God is able to work through to bring about good.

Global Realities of Our Urban World

Consider some of the following points of information about our world today:

- By 2050, the world's urban population is expected to be the same as the total global population of 2002.
- China is expected to have an urban population of 1 billion people by 2050; India will have 0.9 billion.
- Over half of urban dwellers now live in cities or towns with fewer than 500,000 people.
- In 1970 only two megacities (10 million or more inhabitants) existed. Today there are 23 megacities in the world, and 37 are expected by 2025.
- Megacities account for 10 percent of the world's urban population, and 14 percent are expected in 2025.
- There are more people living in the city of Tokyo (37 million) than in the entire country of Algeria, Canada, or Uganda.
- About half of the urban population of the world will live in Asia by 2020.
- Seventy-five percent of the world's urban residents live in 25 countries.
- China, India, and the United States account for 37 percent of the world's urban population.
- The population of the world is expected to exceed 67 percent urban by 2050, with the more developed regions growing from 78 percent urban to 86 percent and the less developed regions from 47 percent to 64 percent.[6]

Amplified Consequences of Sin

Snow is an amazing manifestation of water. Given the right temperature, the moisture in the atmosphere collects and falls to the earth. A single snowflake that lands on the ground concerns no one. However, exponentially increase the number of snowflakes, and several inches (or even feet) of snow pile up, bringing traffic to a stop. When I lived in Kentucky, we would periodically get several inches of snow on our driveway, requiring the use of a shovel. A few minutes of moving only a few inches of snow proved to be a real workout. The concentration of snowflakes, while beautiful to look at on the ground, can halt even the largest of planes, cars, and trucks.

Wherever we find humans in the world (rural, suburban, or urban), we find sin and its consequences. In this sense, the small village is similar to the largest city. As with the snowflakes, the population density found in the urban contexts serves to amplify the effects of sin in a society. The impact of one theft in a small community compared to several hundred in the city brings about a much different outcome. The influence on the social system of a small town with a few unwed, single mothers trying to raise several children is different than hundreds or even thousands of women in similar situations living in the megacity. With a greater concentration of people comes a greater potential for crime. While the percent of robberies in a small community may be the same as that found in a large city, the problems are amplified due in part to the number of thieves committing such acts.

Population

In 1900 the global population was at 1.6 billion people. Only one hundred years later, the population had swollen to 6.1 billion. By 2012, we were on the verge of 7 billion. Another billion is expected to be added by 2025, with 90 percent of the growth coming from developing countries. About 90 percent of the additional population will be in urban areas. Of those in these contexts, one-third will live in slums that lack clean water, proper sanitation, and reasonable housing. The sub-Saharan African context is expected to house 60 percent of its urban dwellers in slums. The pressure of the growing urban populations will apply great strain to countries that are presently unable to care for their people's needs for education, health care, employment, and other necessary infrastructures. By 2015, it is estimated that of the ten largest countries in the world, only one will be in the traditionally Western world.

Countries with the Largest Populations (2015 Estimates)[7]

Rank	Country	Est. Population (millions)
1	China	1,378
2	India	1,247
3	United States	323
4	Indonesia	248
5	Brazil	202
6	Pakistan	194
7	Nigeria	179
8	Bangladesh	176
9	Russian Federation	139
10	Japan	125

Cities tend to be defined by their population densities. According to Robert Neuwirth, "Every year, close to 70 million people leave their rural homes and head for the cities. That's around 1.4 million people a week, 200,000 a day, 8,000 an hour, 130 every minute."[8] Here is a glance at the percentage of people living in the cities by region of the world:

- 40 percent of Africans are living in cities.
- 45 percent of Asians are living in cities.
- 79 percent of Latin America and the Caribbean are living in the cities.
- 71 percent of Oceania are living in cities.
- 73 percent of Europeans are living in cities.
- 82 percent of North Americans are living in cities.[9]

Megacities: Suns in the Solar Systems

I have always been fascinated by astronomy. When I was a child, I received a telescope with a solar viewer attached to it. During the day I was able to point it toward the sun and see sun spots, those cooler areas on the surface with some being larger than the earth in size. At night I was able to see the phases of Venus, the four major moons of Jupiter, and craters within craters on the moon. And though it was evening when viewing these latter astronomical objects, the influence of the sun was still present on all of them. Since planets and moons do not produce their own light, I was only able to view them as the sun shone on them. Also, the gravitational pull of our sun kept those objects in their orbits so I could see them in the evening. The sun's influence on our solar system is great and far-reaching to even our last planet.

Megacities are the suns in the solar systems. Their influences are felt far and wide. Megacites are typically formed as numerous smaller towns and cities come together to create a massive metro area. In 1970 New York and Tokyo were the only two urban agglomerations with at least ten million residents. Twenty years later, the number increased to ten such cities. The following tables show the present number of such megacities and the projected number for 2025. Note the number of such cities existing and arising in the Majority World countries. Also note how the lists are expected to change by 2025.

World's Megacities 2011, 2025[10]

2011		2025	
Megacity	*Population (millions)*	*Megacity*	*Population (millions)*
Tokyo, Japan	37	Tokyo, Japan	39
Delhi, India	23	Delhi, India	33
Mexico City, Mexico	20	Shanghai, China	28
New York-Newark, USA	20	Mumbai (Bombay), India	27
Shanghai, China	20	Mexico City, Mexico	25
São Paulo, Brazil	20	New York-Newark, USA	24
Mumbai (Bombay), India	20	São Paulo, Brazil	23
Beijing, China	16	Dhaka, Bangladesh	23
Dhaka, Bangladesh	15	Beijing, China	23
Kolkata (Calcutta), India	14	Karachi, Pakistan	20
Karachi, Pakistan	14	Lagos, Nigeria	19
Buenos Aires, Argentina	14	Kolkata (Calcutta), India	19
Los Angeles-Long Beach-Santa Ana, USA	13	Manila, Philippines	16
Rio de Janeiro, Brazil	12	Los Angeles-Long Beach-Santa Ana, USA	16
Manila, Philippines	12	Shenzhen, China	16
Moscow, Russian Federation	12	Buenos Aires, Argentina	16
Osaka-Kobe, Japan	12	Guangzhou, Guangdong, China	16
Istanbul, Turkey	11	Istanbul, Turkey	15
Lagos, Nigeria	11	Cairo, Egypt	15
Cairo, Egypt	11	Kinshasa, Democratic Rep. of the Congo	15

World's Megacities 2011, 2025 *(continued)*

2011		2025	
Megacity	Population (millions)	Megacity	Population (millions)
Guangzhou, Guangdong, China	11	Chongqing, China	14
Shenzhen, China	11	Rio de Janeiro, Brazil	14
Paris, France	11	Bangalore, India	13
		Jakarta, Indonesia	13
		Chennai (Madras), India	13
		Wuhan, China	13
		Moscow, Russian Federation	13
		Paris, France	12
		Osaka-Kobe, Japan	12
		Tianjin, China	12
		Hyderabad, India	12
		Lima, Peru	12
		Chicago, USA	11
		Bogotá, Colombia	11
		Bangkok, Thailand	11
		Lahore, Pakistan	11
		London, United Kingdom	10

Diversity

In any given block of a city, one is likely to find the homeless, drug dealers, students, and wealthy elite living side by side. The city is the stewpot where cultures blend together. And though there may be a stereotypical superculture—such as assuming all New Yorkers are unfriendly—much diversity exists. Paul G. Hiebert and Eloise Hiebert Meneses wrote, "We must see the city, therefore, not as a homogenous place, but as hundreds of subcultural groups living and interacting with one another in the same geographic area."[11] This diversity poses a challenge for the church. Methods of evangelism and church planting that work well among the upper-class couples living near the city center may not be as effective in reaching the Guatemalans living three blocks away. Cities require many churches to reach the mosaic of peoples living in them. No single church is able to reach everyone.

Migration

Millions of people living outside of their countries of birth have moved into cities. While places in North America have recently seen more and more immigrants arriving in the suburban contexts, such areas are not divorced from the city. Churches that once found their properties surrounded by a community of people who were ethnically similar to the church now find themselves surrounded by a diversifying context. Though some people migrate with much wealth, others arrive in their new locations with few resources and sometimes knowing only a few people in the new area. Some migrate freely, while others find themselves fleeing for their lives as refugees. Kabul, Islamabad, Delhi, Nairobi, Kuala Lumpur, Cairo, Amman, New York, and Louisville are just a few of the cities that are now the homes to large numbers of refugees. Churches find themselves ministering among people who have a difficult time speaking the language of the majority. Opportunities abound to welcome the strangers next door and provide friendship, language education, and assistance with cultural acquisition. People need to know how to take public transportation, where to shop, how to pay bills, how to use the postal service, and many other tasks that are commonplace for us but not for many migrants.

Poverty

Urbanization is a bittersweet process. It has the potential to improve the quality of life, but the urban contexts also foster much poverty (see chapter 7). While many of the governments of the world have attempted to slow the growth of their slums and improve the quality of life found there, much of the world's population can be found in terrible conditions and progress has not been sufficient to counter the growth rates. These highly visible manifestations of urban poverty are massive in size and are expected to grow in the future. According to the United Nations,

> Over the past 10 years, the *proportion* of the urban population living in slums in the developing world has declined from 39 per cent in the year 2000 to an estimated 32 per cent in 2010. And yet the urban divide endures, because in *absolute* terms the numbers of slum dwellers have actually grown considerably, and will continue to rise in the near future. Between the year 2000 and 2010, the urban population in the developing world increased by an estimated average of 58 million per annum; this includes 6 million who were not able to improve their conditions and joined the ranks of slum dwellers.[12]

Such growth has resulted in one billion people in the world residing in squatter communities. This significant growth will greatly influence the way the church conducts life and ministry in both the present and the future. It is projected that the number of slum dwellers by mid-century will swell to three billion. That is one-third of the estimated global population.[13]

According to the United Nations, a slum household consists of one or more people living under a single roof in an urban context and lacking one or more of the following:

- durable housing (permanent structure providing protections from extreme weather conditions)
- sufficient living area (no more than three people sharing a room)
- access to improved water (water must be sufficient, affordable, and obtainable without extreme effort)
- access to improved sanitation facilities (private toilet, or public toilet shared with a reasonable number of people)
- secure tenure (protection against forced eviction)[14]

Around Karachi and Mumbai a multitude of people live in slums. The massive Kibera slum of Nairobi is one of the poorest areas of the city. While poverty is found in rural and suburban contexts, the cities of the world magnify the issue.

Adila is a mother of four young children. Life in the slum is exceptionally difficult for her. During the day, in addition to caring for the children with their limited food supply, she has to wait in long lines with other women and children to collect water in jerrycans from the community-owned source. Since she and her children are at home all day, they are exposed to harmful fumes of burning trash. Since electricity is nonexistent, cooking takes place indoors with kerosene, adding to the exposure of harmful vapors. Simple tasks, such as the use of a toilet, are taken for granted in much of the Western world but are major concerns that involve thought and planning. Fearing the risk of rape or harassment that may come from walking narrow and dark alleys at night or early morning to the nearest toilet, Adila and her children use plastic bags during these hours. And with Adila left to care for the household waste with a limited water supply for washing and cleaning, she is often exposed to harmful bacteria. While this is a health hazard for her, it is also a hazard for her household as she prepares food.

Adila's story is based on the daily realities of millions of women across the world. Of all the global regions, sub-Saharan Africa has the largest percent of urban dwellers living in slums.

Percent of Urban Residents Living in Slums in 2010[15]

Region	Percent of Urban Population in Slums
North Africa	13
Sub-Sahara Africa	62
South Asia	35
Southeast Asia	31
East Asia	28
West Asia	25
Latin America/Caribbean	24
Oceania	24

Wealth

We are often quick to assume that the urban context is a place exclusively home to poverty. This is not the case. Within the cities of the world, there is a great divide between the poor and the wealthy. The slums of the cities are oftentimes only blocks away from some of the most profitable businesses in the world. For example, in the northern section of Quito, less than 2 percent of the residents are living in poverty. On the south side of the city, the proportion of the population in poverty skyrockets to 95 percent.[16] In addition to the economic divide that is often found in the cities of the world, other divisions manifest themselves in the social, geographical, political, and educational spheres of life. Generally the wealthy have the most social clout, best locations for residence and business, much political power, and access to education. Often with little access to these, the poor remain locked within the world of poverty.

Pace of Change

Change is a constant in the city. While cities may be large with well-developed structures and organizations, life in those cities is marked by change. People transfer jobs. Money becomes scarce, so extended family members move in together. Neighborhoods undergo transitions, and in some cases the costs of living rise and force the poor to move.

Ministering in a context where change is expected poses many difficulties. Churches need to recognize the importance of making disciples and equipping new believers in the Word of God. They need to be taught how to trust in the power of God's Word and the Holy Spirit, for one day they may depart the local church to move to another community. Such opportunities provide the church an avenue to train church planters so that if they depart, the church can work with them to begin making disciples in another area of the city or part of the world.

Urbanization in the United States

Before concluding, I want to direct your attention to the urban contexts in the United States. In the first decade of the twenty-first century, the country's urban population grew faster than the nation's overall growth rate. By 2010 Los Angeles-Long Beach-Anaheim, California, was the most densely populated urbanized area with almost seven thousand people per square mile. The most populous urbanized areas at this time were New York-Newark (eighteen million), Los Angeles-Long Beach-Anaheim (twelve million), and Chicago (nine million). The Charlotte, North Carolina, area had the fastest growth rate for an urbanized area of one million people or more. With almost 95 percent of the population living in the urban areas, California was the most urban state. The states with the largest urban populations were California, Texas, and Florida.[17]

As kingdom citizens, we must never neglect the rural areas, yet as wise stewards in the body of Christ we must recognize that we live in an urban world. The metro area is a different beast than the rural context. Churches, denominations, associations, mission agencies, and networks would be wise to emphasize gospel dissemination and church multiplication across the cities of this country and throughout the world. The cities are the locations of the highest number of people and are the centers of education, business, law, politics, art, science, technology, innovation, and medicine. If the gospel saturates the cities of the world, these realms of influence will be transformed as well. The urban contexts are too diverse, too large, too global, and too significant for the church to attempt to engage the masses with strategies and methods that are difficult to contextualize and reproduce among the people. While the pressure point of the city is a great challenge to the church and her mission, she must not be intimidated by the size, diversity, physical needs, or wickedness found there. The Lord who wept for the city of Jerusalem (Luke 19:41) also died for the nations of the cities. He is not intimidated by the city, so neither should we be. Everything may have begun in a garden, but it will all end in a city (Rev. 21:2).

Questions to Consider

1. Does the city intimidate you? If so, why? What should you do to overcome any fear hindering your church from serving the peoples of the cities?

2. Can you think of any urban challenges not mentioned in this chapter that are hindrances to gospel advancement? What are some practical responses to our mission in light of such issues?

3. Did you grow up in an urban or a rural context? Based on where you grew up, what are the strengths you would bring to serving in the urban contexts? What are the limitations you would bring to serving in the urban contexts?

CHAPTER

9

Children and Youth

*But Jesus said, "Let the little children
come to me and do not hinder them, for to
such belongs the kingdom of heaven."*

—MATTHEW 19:14

When asked about the greatest in the kingdom, Jesus stated, "Truly, I say to you, unless you turn and become like children, you will never enter the kingdom of heaven" (Matt. 18:3). Of all the responses He could have provided, He directed everyone's attention to one of the often overlooked members of society. While not a child, Timothy was encouraged to not allow his youth to become a hindrance but an asset for setting an example before the other believers (1 Tim. 4:12). The Bible makes it clear that children and youth—red, yellow, black, and white—are indeed precious and powerful in His sight.

It is estimated that children under the age of fifteen comprise 26 percent of the world's population.[1] The United Nations identifies youth as those between the ages of fifteen and twenty-four, with this demographic consisting of one billion people in the world.[2] When the categories of children and youth are combined, it is easy to see that individuals in these categories make up a massive number of the global population.

Youth and children are among some of the most neglected, abused, and needy people in the world. War, AIDS, child labor, slavery, prostitution, poverty, and human trafficking have greatly affected many young people of the world. The global diversity of births reveals for every one hundred children born today fifty-five are Asian (nineteen in India, eighteen in China), eight are Latin American and Caribbean, seven are Middle Eastern and North African, sixteen are sub-Saharan African, six are of the Central Eastern Europe/Commonwealth of Independent States and Baltic States, and eight are from the industrialized countries. The church needs to be able to minister to a younger demographic and be prepared for a younger church membership as she makes disciples of all nations. This matter is likely to challenge churches in the West with aging populations. However, such generational issues should not be seen as a hindrance, for the gospel and the kingdom ethic are designed to travel from generation to generation. Our commission did not come with age limitations.

Global Realities

There is no universally agreed-upon definition of *child*, *youth*, or *adult* among the world's governments. The United Nations identifies children as those who are under the age of fifteen, unless a country's laws state otherwise. Stark differences are found among the more and less developed nations of the world when it comes to the number of those under the age of fifteen. In the more developed regions of the world, children comprise 16 percent of the population. In the less developed areas, the number rises to 29 percent. And the number rises to 41 percent in the least developed nations.[3]

The Asia-Pacific region of the world is comprised of 45 percent of the global youth population (seven hundred million). Within this area of the world, South Asia is home to 26 percent of the global youth population. South Asia alone consists of a youth population of 20 percent. Youth living in Southeast Asia and the Pacific area make up 18 percent of the population. The East Asian population consists of 17 percent youth.[4] In Arab regions of the world, youth make up 20 percent of the population, with over half of the population under the age of twenty-five.[5] Africa is the youngest of the continents, with youth making up over 20 percent of the population. It is expected that by 2050 youth will reach 19 percent of the populations in the central, eastern, and western regions of the continent. Southern Africa will be approaching 16 percent, and North Africa 14 percent.[6]

Children and Change in the United States

The United States is presently undergoing demographic shifts among her citizens. In 2011, 24 percent of the United States' population was under eighteen years of age.[7] While the white population is aging, the minority populations not only are younger but have higher fertility rates. Presently, minority groups comprise 37 percent of the US population, a proportion expected to rise to 57 percent in 2060.[8] In almost 20 percent of the US counties, minority children already outnumber white children.[9] Almost one-quarter of elementary and high school students had a parent who was not born in the United States. Twelve million children ages five to seventeen speak a language other than English at home, with nine million of these speaking Spanish.[10]

Most Vulnerable

By far the most vulnerable people in the world are the children and youth. There are numerous situations and people in the world today that, like a roaring lion, are seeking to devour the youth in their communities. Many adults see such young people as a disposable commodity. They are aborted, sold, scorned, and treated as if they do not have any rights as humans. Such hideous realities are nothing new. And even if they are not experiencing harm at the hands of others, they are vulnerable to the problems that often come with unhealthy environments.

Poverty

More than 150 million young workers live in households that are below the poverty line (less than US$1.25 per day). This number represents 24 percent of the total working poor. Out of a desire for work and a better quality of life, many young people are moving to the cities in search of employment. For many this migration means disruption in their social and support networks.[11] Some will arrive to find low-paying jobs and exploitation, and some no available jobs at all.

Education

Many of the world's children do not have the opportunity for a good primary-school level of education. It was noted that in 2008, sixty-seven million primary-school-aged children were not in school.[12] Many children find themselves in contexts where the opportunities for education are limited and very poor at best. The need to work to assist the family often prohibits a child from attending school. Faced with the challenges of the cost of clothes and school supplies, struggling parents find it easier and more helpful to send their children to work to help with life in the city. Situations such as this create a cycle of poverty that traps generations of family members. And in some impoverished contexts, the quality of what little education is available is very poor at best.

Pornography

One government leader from the Philippines stated that the younger the children are, the more saleable they are.[13] This means of sexual exploitation of children and youth is pervasive today. US journalists have done numerous stories on the sharing of child pornography online, with children as young as four and five years of age. Tens of thousands of such photos are posted all the time on social networking sites from people across the globe.

Inequality

While some countries have made great strides in equal rights for children and laws that protect their minorities, much inequality remains. Many people still take advantage of the young, who rarely fight back, know their rights, or know how to voice their abuse to authorities. And of those who speak out against injustices, many authorities are not quick to give much credit to a child's testimony against an adult's persuasive statement.

Street Life and Gangs

It is estimated that 43 percent of children and youth nineteen years old and younger reside in urban areas.[14] While not every child who resides in the urban context is subject to poor living conditions, for many people, such is a reality. The growth of the cities is also resulting in children living and working on the streets. Such a lifestyle opens them up to a life of crime and gangs as well as theft, sexual assault, and violence. Millions of children are forced to flee to the streets. Abuse at home and poverty are often factors that drive children to the streets.

Trafficking

While working on this chapter, I read a recent CNN story on one of the largest operations against human trafficking in Europe. One hundred and three people in ten countries were arrested for smuggling large numbers of people from Afghanistan, Iraq, Pakistan, Syria, and Turkey through the Western Balkan region and Turkey.[15] It is estimated that twenty-seven million men, women, and children are victims of trafficking. There are many manifestations of human trafficking including sex trafficking, child sex trafficking, forced labor, debt bondage, involuntary domestic servitude, forced child labor; and children and youth are often the primary targets of such criminal activity.[16] For example, countless stories have been told of young people being deceived into slave labor and often kidnapped for the sex slave industry. Girls seeking legitimate employment, often to help their struggling families, accept offers to work in other countries, but upon arrival their "employers" reveal that their work involves prostitution. The girls must work for them to repay the costs involved in getting them to the new country. Not having any money to repay the costs for passports (which are usually held by the captors) and other travel expenses, the girls immediately become indebted. If they refuse such work, they are beaten and raped into submission. Consider Alissa's story—reflective of many girls—here in the United States:

> Alissa, 16, met an older man at a convenience store in Dallas and after a few dates accepted his invitation to move in with him. But soon Alissa's new boyfriend convinced her to be an escort for him, accompanying men on dates and having sex with them for money. He took her to an area known for street prostitution and forced her to hand over all of her earnings. He made Alissa get a tattoo of his nicknames, branding her as his property, and he posted prostitution advertisements with her picture on an Internet site. He rented hotel rooms around Dallas and forced Alissa to have sex with men who responded to the ads. The man, who kept an assault rifle in the closet of his apartment, threatened Alissa and physically assaulted her on multiple occasions.[17]

Farshad's account from Tajikistan is another reflection of stories related to illegitimate businesses.

> Farshad, 22, signed a contract with an employment agency in Dushanbe that promised him a well-paid construction job in Russia. The agency also promised to provide housing and three meals a day. The agency's lawyer traveled on the train with Farshad and about 50 other young men, who gave the lawyer money for train tickets, bribes for the customs officials, and migration cards. In four days of travel, the men were given only water. When they arrived in Russia, the lawyer abandoned the group, and the men learned that the agency had not organized any work for them there. Another agency that the men found offered help but then confiscated their passports and sold the men to a local factory director. When the factory director found out some of the workers were planning to escape, he returned their passports only after they agreed to sign statements absolving the firm of any forced labor. Farshad and the others were once again stuck in Russia without work or money to return home.[18]

Child Labor

Some employers see children as a means to their financial ends, and they are willing to do whatever it takes to make money. Children rarely push back against an authority figure. They can be easily manipulated. Of the 2.5 million people in forced labor, it is estimated that 22 to 50 percent are children. In 2008, about 215 million girls and boys (ages five to seventeen) were involved in child labor, with 115 million found to be in hazardous working conditions.[19]

Health Care

Children are often the most susceptible to illness and disease. And poverty only serves as a catalyst to speed up the rate of contracting communicable diseases. Sexually active youth who have not been educated on sexually transmitted diseases are especially prone to contracting and spreading such illnesses. Those who are held captive as sex workers are chronically exposed to an environment that puts their lives at risk. Though progress has been made with decreasing the spread of HIV from mother to child during pregnancy, about one thousand babies were infected each day in 2010 from mother-to-child transmission. Limited access to clean water, proper sanitation, and proper education regarding the threats of disease make for poor health overall. While chapter 10 addresses the pressure point of health care, consider these realities related to the children and youth of the world:

- Almost two million people between ages fifteen and twenty-four die each year from mostly preventable causes.
- Twenty percent of adolescents experience mental health problems each year, mostly depression or anxiety.
- Interpersonal violence takes the lives of about 565 people between the ages of ten and twenty-nine every day.[20]
- In 2008, 40 percent of new HIV infections were among young people between fifteen and twenty-four years of age.
- Eighty percent of young people with HIV live in sub-Saharan Africa, with 70 percent of these being female.[21]
- AIDS or AIDS-related illnesses account for the deaths of more than half of young African females.[22]

In 2010, almost eight million children died before the age of five. The contributing factors in most of these deaths? Pneumonia, diarrhea, or complications during birth. In the case of death by diarrhea, approximately 1.2 million children under the age of five are struck by this grim reality. Vaccine-preventable diseases are prone to outbreaks among populations of children and youth where few are able to obtain basic immunizations. Air quality is also a contributor to the death of many. Each year almost two million children under five years of age die due to polluted indoor air, often as a result of life in the city and dangerous cooking fuels in poorly ventilated areas.[23]

Let Them Come to Me

Sometimes when I speak to groups in the United States on evangelism, I will ask the crowd to raise their hands if they came to faith in Christ before the age of fourteen. A large number of hands always goes up. When I then ask how many of them came to faith before eighteen, it is not unusual for most hands to be in the air.

For some time, studies have repeatedly shown that the majority of believers in the United States come to faith as children. According to researcher George Barna, among those who come to faith in Jesus:

- 43 percent do so before thirteen years of age,
- 64 percent before eighteen years of age,
- 13 percent between eighteen and twenty-one years of age, and
- 23 percent after twenty-one years of age.[24]

While God is not limited by statistics, I do believe that He has revealed there is something strategically critical about sharing the gospel with children and young people. There seems to be a high level of receptivity among America's youth to this good news. We cannot extrapolate from these findings that such is also the case among the young in other cultural contexts. However, these statistics do offer the church much encouragement when it comes to reaching such a demographic anywhere in the world. But above all else, we should remember that Jesus delighted to have children around Him, even rebuking those who were attempting to hinder them from coming to Him (Matt. 19:13–15).

One particular movement among evangelicals makes a strong argument for the need to reach those living within the 4/14 Window. Drawing from the 10/40 Window concept, this play on words represents the timeframe in a person's life when he or she is between four and fourteen years of age, and often believed to be receptive to the gospel. If the findings of the US studies are also reflective of the receptivity levels among children and youth in other countries, then it would be wise stewardship for the church to consider how best to reach those living in this demographic.

Potential Powerhouse for the Kingdom

We often overlook the potential young people have when it comes to making disciples. We are not quick to recognize what the Lord is able to do with this demographic. The church should not be hesitant to minister to the children and youth of the world. As we work with children anywhere in the world, let's keep at least the following two matters in mind.

1. Train and Equip Children and Youth. Young people who enter into the kingdom of God should be equipped to do the work of the ministry just as adults are (Eph. 4:12). They have as much of the Spirit of God as any adult. Helping establish a child on the proper path not only is likely to save him or her from years of sinful living, but can also empower and release another preacher of righteousness into the world. Children and youth are able to reach people whom many adults will never be able to encounter. Their physical and virtual contacts are numerous. There are a multitude of opportunities for the gospel to spread throughout their social networks. Friendships made through schools, sports teams, skate parks, and online connections; and social organizations provide numerous opportunities for the gospel to be communicated to an audience that may not listen to adults.

2. *Cast a Vision for Marketable Degrees and Skills.* Pastors seeking to fulfill their call to equip the saints for the work of the ministry (Eph. 4:11–12) should not overlook the opportunities they have to prepare the young in their congregations for life and mission in the global marketplace. This means beginning with the children—and their parents—and casting a vision for obtaining marketable skills and degrees that would not only help them with a source of income, but would best position them for gospel advancement among the nations of the world. Too often church leaders operate from the perspective that such matters are not in their jurisdiction. However, many opportunities are missed for kingdom expansion by allowing these life-directing decisions to go by the wayside without helping the church consider what is the best stewardship in light of their opportunities and global needs.

Rather than encouraging youth and children to work hard so they can get a good job to earn a living, church leaders need to help their members understand that the Lord's blessings are never to be consumed for personal gain. The Lord does bless His people with the abilities to obtain a good education and provide employment. He ordained work as a good thing. However, achieving the American dream is not a part of God's plan. A culture needs to be created within churches whereby serving the Lord on mission through platforms obtained from marketable skills and degrees is the norm. All of life, including work, is to be for God's glory. Youth and children need to catch such a vision for God's glory and how they are to be involved in making disciples of all nations long before they become adults. Such teaching will assist them in being wise stewards with the opportunities available to them as they move into the marketplace as teachers, mechanics, engineers, biologists, plumbers, and salesmen.

Questions to Consider

1. What level of priority does your church give to making disciples of children? Among those who come to faith, is there a culture that embraces and encourages them for life in the kingdom?

2. Does your church work diligently at equipping parents to shepherd their children wisely? What about helping children grow in their faith in Christ?

3. What do you think the future implications are for missionary teams serving in countries where the present populations are comprised of large percentages of children and youth?

4. Are there ministries that relate primarily to the pressure point of children and youth? What are they, and how will you lead your church to embrace them?

CHAPTER

10

Health Care

But a Samaritan . . . when he saw him,
he had compassion.

—Luke 10:33

Every year, multitudes contract communicable and noncommunicable diseases that affect quality of life. Many of these diseases could be prevented with health education, clean drinking water, proper sanitation, and medical workers. While the greatest need for improved health care is found outside of the West, postindustrialized countries are not exempt from this need. As the church goes into the world, she quickly comes face-to-face with this point of pressure. The challenge is to give water, food, and bandages for wounds while not losing focus on her mission: to make disciples of all nations.

On the day that I was to work on this chapter, Al Jazeera published the following headline: "Measles Outbreak Kills Hundreds in Pakistan." In 2012, 306 children died from measles in the country, five times that of the previous year, when 64 children had died. In the Sindh province, 210 children died in 2012 compared to 28 in the previous year. Health care officials noted that the disease was striking the impoverished areas where families did not vaccinate their children. Many Pakistanis in the rural areas are suspicious of vaccinations, believing they are a Western subversive means to sterilize Muslims. While most people recover from the measles, it can be fatal, especially for malnourished children.[1]

Also on this morning another story caught my attention: "Peru's Amazonian Region Battle Dengue Fever Outbreak." Latin America experienced 161,000 cases of the mosquito-borne virus in 2012. Two-thirds of all deaths related to the disease were among children. No treatment or vaccine for dengue exists. The best preventive measure is to avoid mosquito bites, and that is extremely difficult for people living in the rural Amazonian jungle region.[2]

Historically, the church has been at the forefront of caring for the sick, the discarded, and the suffering. From the adopting of unwanted babies left in the fields to die to the establishment of hospitals, as the kingdom has advanced across the globe and churches have been planted, the care for the physical needs of others has been present as well.

On a related note, as the church has taken the gospel to the nations, many men, women, and children have lost their lives to illnesses contracted while preaching the good news of the Savior who provides healing by His wounds (Isa. 53:5). Numerous lives have been lost to tropical diseases that at the time were unknown in the West. As the church went, many suffered in their bodies. Several years ago, I was part of a church that sent some missionaries on a short-term trip, only to have one contract yellow fever shortly after arriving and spend several days in the hospital once he returned to the States. I have known missionaries who contracted malaria in Southeast Asia, typhoid in Malaysia, and severe intestinal disorders in China and West Africa that caused them to leave their countries of service for an indefinite period of time.

Present Realities

While God's grace has been shown throughout the centuries with great advancements in medicine, sanitation, and better diets, diseases, viruses, and other illnesses will remain a part of this fallen world. The matters of health care will remain to apply pressure on the church, both to the people among whom she ministers and to those she sends to the peoples of the world. Consider the following pressures in our world:

- Malnutrition is the related cause of death in approximately 35 percent of all deaths among children under five years of age.

- In 2011 approximately two-thirds of the deaths of children under five years of age were caused by infectious diseases, pneumonia, diarrhea, malaria, meningitis, tetanus, HIV, and measles.[3]

- Vaccines could prevent about 20 percent of deaths in children under five years of age.

- Almost one-half of the global population is at risk for malaria. Of the 216 million cases in 2010, about 655,000 resulted in death, with 86 percent of these among children five years of age and younger.

- Ninety percent of malaria deaths occur in sub-Saharan Africa.[4]

- In 2010 approximately 2.7 million people were newly infected with HIV.

- By 2010, 34 million people were living with HIV, an increase over previous years.

- There are 17 tropical diseases (with the exception of a couple not prone to outbreak) that affect 1 billion people in 149 countries, causing severe pain, disability, and death.[5]

- In 2010, 2.5 billion people did not have access to improved sanitation facilities, with 72 percent of these living in rural areas.

- Over two-thirds of all cancer deaths occur in low- and middle-income countries. Lung, breast, colorectal, stomach, and liver cancers cause the majority of those deaths.
- Each year 2.8 million die as a result of being overweight or obese.[6]

Life Expectancy

While it has been appointed for people to die (Heb. 9:27), it is clearly lawful to save lives and help those in need (Luke 6:6–11). Though the wages of sin is death (Rom. 6:23), grace and mercy are to be extended to our neighbor in need (Luke 10:25–37). An examination of the regions of the world reveals that life expectancies differ from place to place.

- Twelve percent of the world's population lives in areas where the life expectancy is less than sixty years. Nine percent of the world's population lives in areas where the life expectancy is eighty years or more.
- Between 2045 and 2050, life expectancy in all countries will be over sixty years.
- All areas of the world have experienced major gains in life expectancy in the past sixty years.
- Only Africa has an average life expectancy below seventy years.[7]

The countries with the longest life expectancies can be seen below:

2010–2015 Countries with Longest Life Expectancies[8]

Rank	Country/Area	Life Expectancy
1	Japan	84
2	China, Hong Kong SAR	83
3	Switzerland	83
4	Australia	82
5	Iceland	82
6	Israel	82
7	Italy	82
8	Spain	82
9	France	82
10	Sweden	81

The countries with the lowest life expectancies can be seen below:

2010–2015 Countries with the Lowest Life Expectancies[9]

Rank	Country/Area	Life Expectancy
1	Sierra Leone	48
2	Guinea-Bissau	49
3	Dem. Republic of the Congo	49
4	Lesotho	49
5	Swaziland	49
6	Afghanistan	49
7	Central Africa Republic	50
8	Zambia	50
9	Chad	50
10	Mozambique	51

It should come as no surprise that the nations with the longer life expectancies are the more developed countries with the best medical practices and technology in the world, while those with the lowest numbers are Majority World countries with fewer resources.

Children

When it comes to children and mortality, two measurements are used to indicate well-being and socioeconomic development. *Infant mortality* is the probability of dying between birth and one's first birthday. *Under-five mortality* is the probability of dying between birth and one's fifth birthday. While such mortality rates have been improving in the last sixty years, there are significant differences between more developed and less developed areas of the world.

2010–2015 Infant Mortality Rates[10]

Area	Infant Mortality Rate (deaths per 1,000 live births)
World	42
More Developed Regions	6
Less Developed Regions	46
Africa	71
Asia	37
Europe	6
Latin America/Caribbean	19
Northern America	6
Oceania	19

2010–2015 Under 5 Mortality Rates[11]

Area	Under-Five Mortality Rate (deaths per 1,000 live births)
World	60
More Developed Regions	8
Less Developed Regions	66
Africa	112
Asia	49
Europe	9
Latin America/Caribbean	24
Northern America	8
Oceania	24

While many improvements reduced mortality rates, seven million children died before their fifth birthday in 2011, and on average nineteen thousand still die every day. About half of the under-five deaths in 2011 occurred in the five countries of India, Nigeria, the Democratic Republic of the Congo, Pakistan, and China.[12] Many of these deaths are from causes that could have been prevented with good health care, better nutrition, and basic medicine. Like the table above showing the countries with the lowest life expectancies, the table below points to many developing Majority World countries with limited resources where the highest under-five mortality rates exist.

Countries with the Highest Under-Five Mortality Rates in 2011[13]

Rank	Country	Deaths per 1,000 Live Births
1	Sierra Leone	185
2	Somalia	180
3	Mali	176
4	Chad	169
5	Dem. Rep. of the Congo	168
6	Central African Republic	164
7	Guinea-Bissau	161
8	Angola	158
9	Burkina Faso	146
10	Burundi	139

As a child, I remember being troubled to the point of tears when I saw television commercials seeking money to provide food to the starving children in the world. There has never been a time in my life when I have known hunger or malnutrition. And for most of us, such commercials are simply faces on a screen. The reality is that malnutrition is found in many areas of the world today. It often manifests in a slow breakdown of the body and eventually results in disability and even death. It can even manifest wherever food is present. One relief worker serving among a needy people group was informed that the children in the area were eating their rice; but in the winter they were becoming sick, and many eventually died. The cause was not a lack of food but a lack of vitamins and minerals to sustain healthy life. Rice alone was not sufficient.

Today, one-third of all childhood deaths are attributed to malnutrition. Chronic malnutrition has resulted in the stunted growth of over 40 percent of the children under the age of five in South Asia and sub-Saharan Africa. Once it begins, malnutrition often creates a vicious cycle affecting generations. A malnourished mother gives birth to an underweight baby that is likely to lack the necessary nutrients for proper growth and development. Improper feeding, such as using milk substitutes over exclusive breast milk and the premature use of solid foods, contributes to poor health as well. Less than 40 percent of the children under six months of age living in developing countries receive exclusively breast milk.[14]

Maternal Health

Closely connected to the health of children is the health of their mothers. Malnourished mothers are susceptible to many complications during their pregnancies and often deliver unhealthy children. More than 350,000 women die each year from pregnancy-related causes, with 99 percent of these deaths occurring in developing countries, mostly in South Asia and sub-Saharan Africa. The death of a mother is not just a tragic loss of life but a social and economic burden to a family. Children miss out on the importance of a mother's compassion and instruction. Fathers are left to find a means to care for their children as they seek to provide for them financially (assuming the father did not desert the family).[15]

HIV/AIDS

Since the early 1980s when HIV/AIDS was identified, this infectious disease has become a global destructive epidemic. Left untreated, HIV almost always results in death. Spread primarily through sexual contact, intravenous drug use, and from mother to child, HIV/AIDS has left many orphaned and widowed and has wreaked havoc on the socioeconomic progress of many countries of the world. Each day over 7,400 people contract HIV, and over 5,500 die from AIDS.[16] It is estimated that 34 million people were living with HIV in 2011. As can be noted from the table below, sub-Saharan Africa is the region most affected, with 5 percent of the adult population infected and accounting for 69 percent of people in the world living with HIV.[17] Eighty-six percent of all HIV-positive children live in sub-Sahara Africa.[18]

Countries Most Affected by HIV Infections, 2009[19]

Country	HIV estimated percentage in 2009 among those 15–49 years of age
Swaziland	26
Botswana	25
Lesotho	24
South Africa	18
Zimbabwe	14
Zambia	14
Namibia	13
Mozambique	12
Malawi	11
Uganda	7

Though the number of newly infected cases has decreased worldwide, increases have occurred in the Middle East, North Africa, Eastern Europe, and Central Asia. While the number of AIDS-related deaths has been declining since the mid-2000s, two million still occurred in 2011. The church in these areas of the world must continue to face the challenges of ministering to families with members who have contracted HIV, both within the church membership as well as those in the community. Serving children whose parent or parents have died from AIDS or AIDS-related causes will continue to be a reality.

Sanitation and Clean Water

Years ago, my grandfather developed a successful septic tank-cleaning business from which he retired. When asked what I thought of his job, I said, "It stinks!" He did not appreciate my sense of humor. But many people appreciated his work. In much of the Western world, we take matters such as waste disposal for granted. I know I do. Growing up around my grandfather's business, cleaning septic systems was a regular part of discussion and life in southeastern Kentucky. When I moved away to college and later married, Sarah and I lived in a city and were on the public sewage system. There has never been a time in my life when I have been concerned about the potential health hazards related to septic system matters.

Consider garbage disposal. I have never feared that my trash would build up to a point that it would become a haven for disease-carrying animals. I have always known of plastic garbage bags, trash containers, and weekly (and sometimes biweekly) trash collectors. In fact, I rarely think about such matters. I have lived in four different cities and never known where the local garbage dump was located. I simply put out the trash, and it disappears forever.

Water is required for proper health. Without it, people die. We consume it in various forms. As I write this paragraph, I have a cup of coffee sitting next to me on my desk in my office. At my house a plumber is working on a sink in my bathroom from which I plan to get water tonight before bed. I have never had to be concerned about the quality of my drinking water or the challenges of obtaining it.

Most of us simply flush our waste away and give our trash to trash collectors to carry away; whenever we need a drink, we simply turn on a faucet to bring the water to us. For 2.6 billion people in the world, such conveniences are not reality. In fact, not only do they lack the luxury of being able to flush a toilet or turn a spigot, but they have to deal with the 24/7 realities of open sewers flowing through their streets and in front of their doorways, and long walks to get water that is not necessarily safe for consumption. While in developing countries the percent of those with access to improved sanitation grew between 1990 and 2008, more than 40 percent of these 2.6 billion people practice open defecation.[20]

Rapid population growth, industrialization, growth of the cities, and agricultural needs will continue to strain the available freshwater supply on the earth. Of all the water on the planet, only 2.5 percent is freshwater. It is expected that the world's population facing water shortages will increase more than fivefold by 2050. In 2008, the following countries had the lowest access to clean water sources:

- Somalia
- Ethiopia
- Papua New Guinea
- Madagascar
- Dem. Rep. of the Congo
- Mozambique
- Afghanistan
- Niger
- Mauritania
- Sierra Leone[21]

* * *

Sarah, my wife, is a physician who specializes in internal medicine and pediatrics. Ever since medical school, she wanted to serve a needy population in the United States. When we lived in Louisville, Kentucky, she worked part-time at a clinic for the uninsured population in the area. After we moved to Birmingham, the Lord also opened an opportunity for her to serve a similar population. While the health care debate continues in the United States, we must recognize that even among those without insurance, what is here is much better than what is found in many areas of the world. Even for the uninsured, something is available to assist them to some degree.

In the West we also periodically hear of public sanitation problems, water quality issues, and illnesses. While I do not want to make light of the challenges to health and quality of life in the Western world, I do want to draw attention to this global pressure point. The church on mission will face these realities as she serves and labors to make disciples of all nations. If missionary teams are being sent from developed countries, then part of their training should be an awareness of such enormous challenges, terrible disease, and ever-present death.

In light of the gravity of global needs, the church must never lose sight of her mission to make disciples of all nations, while serving those suffering. John Piper rightly reminds us that "Christians, Bible believing people, care about all suffering, especially eternal suffering."[22] Whatever the responses are to the specific, local realities of our neighborhood children with poor drinking water, malnourished pregnant mothers, and fathers too sick to work, we must care about the whole person, not just the physical needs. If the church helps those in need without calling them to repentance and faith in Christ alone, then the church in that area is no more than a social relief organization attempting to provide temporary relief to people about to experience eternal suffering! We offer the cup of water, even if they do not want to follow Jesus. We provide bread, even if they refuse the good news. If we believe the Bible and fill the belly but never give them a chance to have their hearts filled, then we are among the cruelest people in the world.

Questions to Consider

1. What are some of the health care needs in your community?

2. How can you and your church be involved in caring for those with physical needs as you share the gospel? Even if your church does not have any physicians, nurses, dentists, or other traditional health care employees, what resources do you have that may serve those in need?

3. As your church sends missionaries into other contexts where there are great physical needs, how is your church equipping them for life and mission in light of the pressure point of health care?

4. How will you and your church stay focused on making disciples of all nations in light of the great physical needs that you will encounter as you go?

11

Oral Learners

Faith comes from hearing.

—ROMANS 10:17

During the mid-fifteenth century, a new form of technology was being used that would bring literature to the masses. German inventor Johann Gutenberg had been experimenting with a printing press that used replaceable and movable letters. One historic day, using such movable type, he would produce the world's first book—the Bible—and would change the world.

For the next five hundred years, his invention defined the world of publishing. However, it was the Bible itself that would forever change the way the world thought about the Christian faith. As it has been said, from that moment on the Christian faith has walked on literate legs. While such a declaration is a bit of an overstatement—the faith once for all delivered to the saints has always been a literate-based faith as God often told His servants to write what He revealed—there is much truth in this use of hyperbole.

Throughout the centuries, as the gospel advanced, so has literacy. The church has often brought the good news to people, along with reading skills so that those they minister to would be able to better comprehend the Bible. Among some peoples whose languages have never been written, missionaries have been at the forefront of developing a written expression of the spoken word, followed by instruction in how to read the new system of markings, letters, and symbols.

137

The gospel and growth in Christ has always been for both the literate and the illiterate. As long as someone has been able to teach faithfully the truth of the Scriptures, people come to faith in Jesus and can walk in obedience to Him. And while such language development, translation, and literacy efforts are important, many of the world's people are functionally illiterate. The pressure on the church for years to come is that of understanding how best to evangelize, plant churches, and teach obedience to those who are described as oral learners.

Present Global Realities

About four billion people in the world are oral communicators, people "who can't, don't, or won't take in new information or communicate by literate means."[1] Author and professor emeritus Tex Sample, writing almost twenty years ago, commented on orality matters both within the United States and throughout the world: "It is my contention that about half of the people in the United States are people who work primarily out of a *traditional orality*, by which I mean a people who can read and write—though some cannot—but whose appropriation and engagement with life is oral. More than this, I am convinced that most churches have a clear majority of their membership who work from a traditional orality." When one moves outside the United States into most of the rest of the world, the mass of oral cultures, both primary and traditional, looms even larger. Two-thirds of the people in the world are oral.[2]

Among the languages of the world, a surprisingly small percentage have even been written. Walter Ong, in his influential work *Orality and Literacy*, notes that "of all the many thousands of languages—possibly tens of thousands—spoken in the course of human history only around 106 have ever been committed to writing to a degree sufficient to have produced literature, and most have never been written at all. Of the some 3000 languages spoken that exist today only some 78 have a literature."[3] And while this may surprise those of us in the Western world where reading and books are commonplace, a more surprising reality is that possibly 90 percent of the world's Christian workers are sharing the gospel using highly literate communication styles such as printed literature and an "expositional, analytical and logical presentation of God's word."[4] In other words, many people are using methods primarily designed for those who read in order to share the gospel with oral learners.

Orality

Since you are reading this book, you are highly literate in your way of communication. Literate learners think in terms of words, the application of principles, and organization that flows in one direction. Before I started writing chapters in this book, I developed a chapter outline with major and minor points. We think in terms of propositional truth and logical order. All of these are good and important. And when it comes to making disciples of all nations, we are to teach people propositional truth from God's Word and how to divide the Word rightly.

Orality is reliance on the spoken word rather than the written word. In oral societies storytelling, proverbs, riddles, dances, festivals, poems, and songs are many of the primary means of communication, instruction, and connecting with the past. According to orality specialist Grant Lovejoy, "Orality will be a factor in missions strategy for the next half a century."[5] As the primary means of communication among oral peoples, the church must learn how to communicate the never-changing truth found in the Scriptures using such methods.

And here is the challenge: we imitate what we know, and we know what has been modeled before us. Therefore, if we have been taught a predominately literate worldview that emphasizes linear thought and logic, and have been taught how to think and communicate within that same worldview, then we will have to learn how to function as translators—filtering the biblical truths through our literate framework and into the world of the oral learner.

Though the discussions surrounding the pressure point of oral learners have been increasing in recent years, I do not wish to presume that everyone reading this book is familiar with such conversations. Therefore, the following definitions are provided to give clarity to understanding the nomenclature that has developed among missionaries working with oral learners.

Oral Preference: Having a preference for receiving and processing information in an oral format rather than print. The person may or may not be a reader.

Primary Oral Culture: Cultures with no knowledge at all of writing.

Secondary Oral Communicators: People who depend on electronic audio and visual communications.

Residual Orality: Description of those who have been exposed to literacy, even learned to read, but retain a strong preference for learning by oral means rather than literate means.

Aliteracy: A lack of interest in or enjoyment of reading; characteristic of people who are capable of reading with understanding but do not often read for pleasure.

Bible Storying: A generic term that includes the many forms of telling Bible stories, of which chronological Bible storying is the main format.

Chronological Bible Storying: A method of sharing biblical truths by telling the stories of the Bible as intact stories in the order that they happened in time.

Chronological Bible Storytelling: The act of presenting biblical truth generally in story format though the story may be deeply paraphrased or may be interrupted for teaching whenever some important issue occurs in the passage. The story may or may not be kept intact as a story. It follows a chronologically organized timeline.

Chronological Bible Teaching: The type of chronological Bible instruction used by New Tribes Mission, popularized by Trevor McIlwain in the 1970s. It references biblical stories but does not necessarily tell them as intact stories. It uses exposition and explanation as teaching approaches. This method presupposes at least semi-literacy on the part of the teacher.[6]

Categories of Learning

Another set of terms developed to assist in understanding the global realities of this pressure point relate to the different degrees of literacy. Missiologist James B. Slack has written extensively on the topic of orality and Bible storying. According to Slack, there are five primary categories of learning abilities as related to literacy and orality. All five can be found throughout the world.[7]

Primary Illiterates: Individuals in this category are unable to read or write. Written words simply appear as meaningless scribbles. For them, words form pictures in their minds. Those in this category are oral communicators, relying on stories to communicate.

Functional Illiterates: Those in this category have started to read and write within a school context. However, they do not progress beyond the eighth grade. They can read simple texts, but cannot recall or reproduce what they read. Values come from stories, not literate means. Though classified as literate, such individuals learn primarily through oral means of communication.

Semi-literates: In most countries, individuals in this category would have either progressed to the tenth or twelfth grade, depending on the school system. They are in a transitional stage from being primarily oral learners to primarily literary learners. Semi-literates learn best and are the most comfortable with oral methods of communication.

Functional Literates: Those in this category are literate learners. Precepts, ideas, principles, and concepts are understood.

Highly Literates: These individuals are a part of a word-culture. They often spend time each day reading and writing. They are literate communicators.

Part of effective gospel communication and church multiplication among the nations is understanding where the people being served tend to fall in these categories and then determining the proper methods of communication. As followers of Christ, we are not only students of His Word but also students of the peoples to whom He sends us. Knowing one's context is critical to the mission, and understanding context involves understanding how best to communicate with the people so they may come to an understanding of the truth.

Faith Comes by Understanding

This past Christmas season, my family and I watched our usual collection of holiday cartoons. Of course the

Charlie Brown specials are near the top of our list. While the children are easily understood in these shows, the voices of the adults are unintelligible to the at-home viewers. Remember Charlie Brown's teacher? You never see her, but there is a sound for her voice. *Waaa Waa Wa, Waaa Wa Waa.* That muted trombone sound is clearly heard but cannot be understood.

Throughout the Scriptures, it is clear that simply hearing words is not sufficient for repentance and faith in Christ. There must be understanding. Yes, faith comes by hearing (Rom. 10:17), but such hearing involves recognition of the propositional truth and story that is shared. Belief in the heart (Rom. 10:9) is not possible without knowledge. Therefore we read of Paul seeking prayer for opportunities to proclaim the gospel but with a desire that it should be communicated with clarity (Col. 4:3–4). While it is important for us to communicate the truth of the Scriptures to others, we must make sure our audiences understand what they hear—or read. Providing them with words, either on a page or verbally, is not sufficient. We must communicate in a contextually appropriate way that connects with our hearers.

Gospel advancement among the Tiv tribe in Central Nigeria is an example of the challenges of approaching a primarily oral society with literacy-based methods instead of oral methods. For twenty-five years missionaries worked among the Tiv and saw an average of one person per year come to faith in Jesus and experience baptism. The missionaries used a preaching style they had learned in Bible school as the way to evangelize. However, after some of the Tiv believers started setting the gospel story to musical chants—which were a common means of communication for them—the gospel quickly advanced with the numbers of new believers surging to 250,000. The people had been hearing, but *not understanding.*[8]

As the church continues to serve in the twenty-first century, she will continue to face the pressure of oral learners. Faithful kingdom service requires we meet such people where they are rather than expecting them to meet us where we are. If our Lord incarnated Himself among us (John 1:14; Gal. 4:4) and calls us to follow Him into the world, then we must also leave our comfort zones as we share His story with others so that their story may intersect with His.

Questions to Consider

1. Prior to reading this chapter, had you ever heard of oral learners or Bible storying? If so, what was the context where you encountered such thoughts?

2. What can you and your church do now to better prepare yourselves for making disciples and multiplying churches among oral learners?

3. While the Bible consists of many stories that can easily be told, the Epistles are not in a story format. How could you teach an oral learner the truths of the Epistles?

4. Do you see any possible dangers when it comes to using stories, poems, and music to evangelize and teach others the truths of the Bible? If so, what are they, and how can they be avoided?

12

Pornification of Societies

Flee from sexual immorality.

—1 Corinthians 6:18

One of the global pressure points influencing the church and mission today is that of sexual immorality. While few discussions link this matter to the challenge of making disciples of all nations, this is a topic that needed to be included as a pressure point.[1] The pornification of societies refers to the grip of sexual immorality on people both within the kingdom and outside the kingdom. In our hypersexualized contexts, the business of pornography is big business. The reach of such evil is significant, both far and wide.

While attempting to discern whether or not this topic warranted a chapter in this book, the obvious question was, Is the presence and impact of pornography so widespread that its influence is shaping the face of the church today? At first, I was not convinced that it was; however, the more I read and listened to others, the more I came to believe that this is a major issue impacting the making of disciples of all nations.

There were two matters when considering this topic that I wanted to avoid. First, I did not want to create a mountain out of a molehill. I did not want to make the claim or give the impression that the influence of pornography was greater than what it is. If in reality it was not as pervasive as some strongly believe, then I did not want to go along with any argument that may be based on an antiporn passion rather than reality. Zeal may be good, but zeal without knowledge is not good (Prov. 19:2). If this topic was to be included in this book, then reality had to justify its inclusion as a chapter.

Second, I did not want to include this sinful matter in this book if it would give the impression that pornography is worse than another sin. Sin is sin whether it is stealing a candy bar or murder. Clearly the influence and ramifications of sin differ. The social repercussions for stealing a piece of candy rightly differ from taking innocent life.

There are many habitual sins that run rampant across the globe: outbursts of anger, hatred, drug and alcohol addictions, greed, lying, and many others. So I had to ask, What makes this issue so substantial that it should be included in this book as opposed to another sinful matter? And as I began to research the issue of pornography, I came to understand that there is a massive industry and extensive technology supporting it. Such systems and organizations do not exist for the promotion of many of the sins common to people. With pornography comes a multibillion-dollar industry with global strategies designed to facilitate and promote sexual immorality. Yes, the influence of the manufacturing and selling of drugs is extensive across the globe, but a person cannot simply click on a Web site and partake of such material.[2]

I also began to talk with counselors, pastors, and other church and mission-agency leaders about their thoughts on this topic. While my discussions and correspondence took place with those from differing contexts and ministries, I was surprised to hear they felt that pornography is now a major issue in the church as well as among potential missionary candidates. Many are now assuming—especially among men—that missionary candidates have used pornography unless told otherwise. When such an expectation—particularly within the church—is commonplace, we find ourselves living in a pornified society.

Sarah and I have a wooded lot behind our house that is covered with ivy. Since we live in an older house, I would estimate that this plant has been growing for about fifteen to twenty years without any pruning. When we purchased the house, we noticed a small area that was fenced and was likely the home for a dog. The ivy had crept over, around, and through the fence, making the area an eyesore. One weekend we decided the time had come for us not only to clear out some of the ivy that was on the ground, but also to dismantle and remove the fence. With several tools in hand, we went to work. The ivy that had covered the area was so entwined with the metal fence that we had to cut the plant at the ground level to remove the fencing. And even after the ivy was cut, it was extremely difficult to separate the walls of the fence, for the vine had encased the walls. After a very lengthy period of cutting the plant and removing bolts, we finally had the walls separated. However, as we tried to pull the fencing across the ground to dispose of it, the bottom of the fence continued to get caught in the ivy that carpeted the ground. It was as if the plant did not want to let go and desired to hold the fence captive.

Pornography is a satanic creature that also has extensive tentacles which creep into a multitude of areas of life, often slowly weaving their way in to the point of taking people captive. Pornography leads to the development of a worldview, an ideology, that shapes the way people understand themselves, other men and women, children, God, relationships, masculinity and femininity, and obviously sexual relations.

In the first chapter of Romans, which describes the sinful depravity of all people, before Paul mentions numerous sinful acts that manifest themselves from our sin natures, sexual immorality is described first and with more detail, noting the gravity of such sinfulness:

> Therefore God gave them up in the lusts of their hearts
> to impurity, to the dishonoring of their bodies among

themselves, because they exchanged the truth about God for a lie and worshiped and served the creature rather than the Creator, who is blessed forever! Amen.

For this reason God gave them up to dishonorable passions. For their women exchanged natural relations for those that are contrary to nature; and the men likewise gave up natural relations with women and were consumed with passion for one another, men committing shameless acts with men and receiving in themselves the due penalty for their error.

And since they did not see fit to acknowledge God, God gave them up to a debased mind to do what ought not to be done. They were filled with all manner of unrighteousness, evil, covetousness, malice. They are full of envy, murder, strife, deceit, maliciousness. They are gossips, slanderers, haters of God, insolent, haughty, boastful, inventors of evil, disobedient to parents, foolish, faithless, heartless, ruthless. Though they know God's righteous decree that those who practice such things deserve to die, they not only do them but give approval to those who practice them (Rom. 1:24–32).

The bride of Christ is a supernatural body, empowered by the Supernatural. We are called to be Spirit-filled (Eph. 5:18) and not quench the Spirit (1 Thess. 5:19). Local churches are not to tolerate sexual immorality among their members and should not associate with "sexually immoral people" who claim to be brothers or sisters in the Lord. And any such person claiming to be a member of the church is to be removed from the fellowship of the body (1 Cor. 5:9–13).

The Size of the Industry

Gone are the days in the United States when pornography was stigmatized by the masses as something dirty. No more driving across town to the other side of the tracks or walking up dark alleys under the cloak of darkness to venture into some seedy shack selling magazines and videos. Pornography is now mainstream. Whether it is *Fifty Shades of Grey* selling twenty million copies in the United States (forty million worldwide),[3] large billboards for "gentlemen's clubs" on the sides of interstates, or apps providing access to a wealth of free pornography, smut is readily available in copious amounts—in an instant. Kids no longer have to plan their week around how they may be able to obtain a quick glimpse of a stolen pornographic magazine; now many are often exposed to such wickedness while doing homework on their tablets or computers.

Pornography has become fashionable, expected, the source for comedy. It is accepted. And the more commonplace it becomes, the more the people will demand edgier material to satisfy the craving that is no longer satisfied by what is mainstream. Space will not permit me to discuss the historical and cultural shifts regarding how pornography has moved from smoke-filled grungy movie houses and peep show booths of decades gone by to now being on demand in upscale hotel chains, as nearby as one's smartphone, and even being consumed in the workplace. So I will simply make the statement that within the United States, pornography has moved from seclusion to the open.

Pornography is big business. In 2006, the revenues from the sex and pornography industry in the United States were larger than those of the NFL, NBA, and MLB combined.[4] It is no longer an underground set of operations. The pornography industry involves corporations as well as the single videographer with a camera. It involves managers and mergers. Companies have accountants and Human Resource departments. A report in 2007 cited that there were eight hundred million rentals of adult videos in US stores that year, the existence of a trade organization representing nine hundred companies in the pornography business, and that Americans were spending around $10 billion per year on pornography. Also, it was estimated that the industry employed over twelve thousand people in California alone, with the industry in that state paying over $36 million in taxes that year.[5] Magazines, movies, games, Web sites, and photos are just some of the means by which pornography is distributed.

Reliable statistics are difficult to obtain, especially with the rise of "amateur porn" (particularly for free viewing). It is nearly impossible to know the precise numbers. Therefore, while I share the following statistics with some reservation—not knowing with clarity the research methods used to gather the data—I have noticed that many journalists, ministries, and sociologists are also referencing such numbers, or ones close to these. While one writer made the argument of a much smaller pornography economy than what the majority are claiming, even his figure was a few billion dollars in size.[6]

Pornography is massive in its availability and reach. Many people, including academics, reference Jerry Ropelato's article, "Internet Pornography Statistics." According to Ropelato's extensive compilation of figures:

- $3,075.64 is being spent on pornography every second.
- 28,258 users are viewing pornography every second.
- Every 39 minutes a new pornographic video is being produced in the United States.
- Global pornography revenues equal $97 billion, with the industry being larger than the combined revenues of Microsoft, Google, Amazon, eBay, Yahoo!, Apple, Netflix, and EarthLink.[7]

As the pornography business has grown and developed, other businesses—including nonpornography-related ones—often find themselves in business partnerships making a profit from porn. Such corporate interactions continue to lend support and momentum that such business is legitimate. For example, after examining the gigantic amounts of data transfer from some of the largest online pornography sites, Ashlee Vance, writing for *Bloomberg Businessweek*, noted, "My takeaway from this is that companies such as Dell and Cisco Systems make a ton of money selling gear to the top porn sites and that these companies must have some very savvy engineers."[8] Whether it is providing software and hardware resources directly to pornographers or international hotel chains carrying pay-per-view "adult entertainment" with titles guaranteed not to show up on the hotel bill, the reality is that what was once described as "filth" is now legitimate, expected, and mainstream.

The Global Reach

I once was talking with a young man about his struggle with pornography. For some time he had been addicted to it, but through God's grace had overcome this burden and was now helping other men turn away from the guilt and sin attached to it. He spoke of how it had affected him, his view of women, and his relationship with his fiancée. While I was saddened at what he had experienced, I was very thankful for the forgiveness, restoration, and liberation he had experienced in Christ. Wanting to get his perspective on this plague on societies, I asked him why he thought it was such a problem today. "Because it is everywhere," he immediately replied. "I can pull it up on my phone right now. It is all around us."

This brother's story is not unique. Many men—and also women—within the church are struggling with the seduction of pornography. And one of the reasons for this impact is that it is truly everywhere in an instant.

The three largest pornography sites in the world each receive over two billion page views per month, with the largest over four billion.[9] It has been estimated that 43 percent of Internet users view pornography.[10] While it is often stated that 90 percent of the world's pornography can be traced back to San Fernando, California, the reach of such material is fascinating. It is estimated that 12 percent (twenty-five million) of all websites are pornographic, with forty million Americans alone as regular viewers. Seventy percent of men between the ages of eighteen and twenty-four visit pornography sites each month. Sixty-eight million daily search engine requests are related to pornography, and 35 percent of all downloads are pornographic.[11]

It has been reported that each day, sixty million people view pornography on the world's largest free pornography site.[12] While pornographers have always been at the forefront of technological advances—be they photography, motion pictures, videos, video games, web cameras, or pay-per-view—to disseminate their material, the Internet has allowed a very large business to become ubiquitous overnight.

Regarding search engines, in 2006 South Africa, Ireland, and New Zealand led the way in searches using *porn* as the keyword; Bolivia, Chile, and Romania with *xxx*; and Pakistan, India, and Egypt with *sex*. The United States, Brazil, the Netherlands, Spain, and Japan are the world's largest producers of pornographic videos. In 2006, $27 billion was spent in China on pornography and $25 billion in South Korea. There are 245 million pornographic web pages connected to the United States, 10 million in Germany, and 8.5 million in the United Kingdom.[13]

Pornography knows no geographical, ethnic, gender, or even religious boundaries. Japanese pornography is popular in Indonesia. Two developing enterprises are found in Ghana and in Nairobi, Kenya. African and Uzbek leaders are upset over the development of pornography in their areas. And pornography is popular in Afghanistan as leaders attempt to prevent it from being accessible at Internet cafes.[14] In 2012 the Muslim world was humiliated when the numbers revealed that pornographic sites were among the most visited sites in Egypt, Tunisia, and Lebanon.[15] News from Pakistan was not encouraging either when in 2010 Google ranked the country number one in the world in searches for pornographic terms.[16]

And with piracy and the black markets of the world, videos are even influencing peoples living in remote areas. One news reporter traveled to a village in Ghana where people lived in huts but still were able to watch pornographic movies. When the reporter asked how this was possible, he was told that the men and boys would gather in a hut and watch American-made videos while running a generator to produce the necessary power. And it was in this village that some of the younger men had attempted to imitate what they saw on the television, with one man stating he had raped a girl and another man in a different location bemoaning the fact that he had contracted HIV by practicing what he had learned from American videos.

The Influence of Pornography

As people have become more and more desensitized to the images of pornography over the past fifty years, the demand for more perverse, bizarre, and edgy images and actions has grown. The *Playboy* images of the 1960s are now the stuff found on the covers of women's magazines in the grocery store checkout lines. Pornography plays to the human desire like a drug. The sensation that comes from using pornography eventually reaches a level of tolerance, so a different set of images are necessary to produce the high. As consumers have requested more and more provocative pornography, the producers have willingly complied in order to sell a product. Just as the raising of the water lifts all the boats to a new level, a couple of generations of consumers over the course of several decades has facilitated the depth of the depravity manifest in today's pornography, bringing it to a new level of evil across mainstream societies. In an interview with Eleanor Hall, feminist and professor of sociology and women's studies at Wheelock College, Gail Dines, illustrated this point based on her research:

> ELEANOR HALL: You've been studying pornography for more than two decades. Are you shocked by the sort of Internet porn that is readily available?
>
> GAIL DINES: I have to tell you, I am actually shocked, yes, that it got so bad so quickly. I mean, if you were to tell me, 15 years ago, that we would be seeing images like this, I would've thought not possible.
>
> And what I'm also incredibly shocked at is how the pornographers have come in and done a kind of self-attack on the culture, and there's been no mass movement against it.
>
> I mean, I think if parents understood what their children are being bombarded with, I think they'd be really angry and upset, because it undermines their ability to socialise their children.[17]

This influence impacts a multitude of ages. The thirty-five to forty-nine-year-old demographic is the largest consumer of pornography online. Ten percent of adults admit to an Internet sexual addiction. And while men obviously get the most attention whenever it comes to the use of pornography, they are not the only consumers. In general, one in three visitors to pornographic websites are women, with 17 percent of women admitting to struggling with a pornography addiction in general. Among the general population, 34 percent of Internet users receive unwanted exposure to pornographic material. Presently, the average age of the first Internet exposure to pornographic material is eleven.[18]

Temptations That Abound

More men (28 percent) admit to being tempted to view pornography or sexually inappropriate material online than women (8 percent). The Milliennial generation (27 percent) is more likely to be tempted to view online pornography than Generation X (22 percent) or Baby Boomers (15 percent). The Milliennials are also more likely to be tempted by other sexual opportunities. Twenty-one percent of them admit they are often tempted to do something sexually inappropriate with someone, as compared to Generation X (11 percent) and Baby Boomers (5 percent).[19]

The evidence within the church is not encouraging either. In 2001, *Leadership Journal* released some numbers from their research. Of pastors polled at the time, 6 percent agreed that they had visited a pornographic Web site a couple of times a month or more; 21 percent had a few times a year; 9 percent had one visit in the last year; 7 percent had made such a visit more than a year ago. Fifty-seven percent stated that they had never visited a pornographic web site.[20] In 2006, ChristiaNet took a poll of one thousand responses and concluded that 50 percent of Christian men and 20 percent of Christian women in their study had problems with pornography.[21] Mike Genung, director of a ministry to those with sexual struggles, also estimates that half of the men in churches have a problem with pornography.[22] In a 2003 study of 1,024 US adults, Barna found that 38 percent of Americans approve of pornography. Among evangelicals 7 percent believed it was morally acceptable to have a sexual relationship with someone of the opposite sex with whom the person is not married, and 5 percent believed it was morally acceptable to look at pictures of nudity or explicit sexual behavior. When Barna inquired among those who were "born again" but did not consider themselves to be evangelical, 35 percent believed it was morally acceptable to have a sexual relationship with someone of the opposite sex with whom the person is not married, and 28 percent believed it was morally acceptable to look at pictures of nudity or explicit sexual behavior.[23]

Prior to working on this chapter, I spent time talking with church and denominational leaders, asking them about the present influence of pornography on the missionaries they are equipping, interviewing, and sending into the world to make disciples. A few church leaders shared that almost every college-aged man with whom they have worked is struggling with the lure of pornography or has had a past problem with it. Counselors and representatives of mission agencies shared with me that they have seen an increase in the number of men who are struggling with pornography as compared to men a few years ago.

Unfortunately, over the past decade, I have known of brothers and sisters who have had to resign from positions of leadership because of matters related to the use of pornography in their lives. A simple online search reveals that over the past several years, many former church leaders have been removed from shepherding churches because of pornography—with some being arrested because of their possession of child pornography. And while such matters have been unfolding at home, the mission field struggles too. Any time someone is serving as a leader in the church, the spiritual opposition is great. Such opposition is even more intense for those who are laboring on the edge of the kingdom's advancement into darkness. Jim Lo has noted the lure and deceptive nature of pornography. One missionary shared with him the following personal story:

> One day I was on the Internet looking up some information for a new ministry I was thinking about starting. As I was surfing through the different sites I unintentionally happened onto an X-rated site. Understand

me, I was not purposefully looking for pornography, but the images tempted me to want to see more. It was the first time in months that I felt any sort of emotion. I felt "alive" once again.

Every time I needed a shot to fill the emotional vacuum in my life I went to my computer. I reasoned that it was my reward for having given so much of myself in ministry. "God will forgive. All the good I am doing as a missionary far outweighs a few moments of looking at naked people."

The grip of guilt tightly squeezed my heart, but I was trapped. The more tired I got the more I began depending upon pornography to get an emotional fix. It was horrible. The guilt feelings, mixed with the temporary feelings of pleasure, made me feel like Dr. Jekyl and Mr. Hyde. My effectiveness as a missionary decreased as I sought to live the double life. My family life also suffered. It took me almost losing everything before I came to my senses and realized that I was allowing pornography to hurt myself, my family and my ministry.[24]

The Biblical Realities

Arguments abound both for and against pornography. Those within the pro category might say, "As long as no one gets hurt, it does not matter if someone looks at porn or not," or—as I once heard a college professor say—"Pornography is good because it is designed as a sexual education tool." Some argue that pornography provides men a sexual escape so that they avoid turning those pent-up sexual urges on children or raping women. Others argue that it is good for marriages when one partner is not satisfied with the other, but does not want to have an affair or get a divorce. Contrarily, it has been reported that 47 percent of Christians stated that pornography is a major problem in the home.[25]

Some of the most outspoken opposition to pornography comes from feminists who recognize that pornography degrades women, creates in men and women an unhealthy and unrealistic notion of sex, creates a culture that accepts and promotes rape, is supported by an industry that cares little for the sex worker, and results in erectile dysfunction in men because they are sensitized to sex always being an unrealistic fantasy. Many have argued that pornography has created a culture divorcing sex from relationship. Many young men would rather masturbate to pornography than experience sexual activity in the context of the complexities of relationships. Pornography has helped men become lazy and irresponsible. Pornography also contributes to promiscuity, infidelity, sexual addiction, prostitution, human trafficking, pedophilia, rape, and even murder.

While I recognize that not everyone who looks at pornography will become an addict, pedophile, rapist, or murderer, such outcomes of sin are not the point I am trying to make. And while there are many outstanding arguments—both within and outside the church—as to the malignancy of pornography, the reality is that the Bible condemns sexual immorality.

Whether or not the business of porn is several billion more than the conservative estimates state, the women in the business are being abused, or porn has no effect on someone's cognitive and social functions; the bottom line—among all of the arguments—is that fornication, lust, and adultery are sins.

God created sex. It is a very good thing and an amazing gift. It is for pleasure, procreation, and strengthening the relationship between a husband and a wife. However, like any other blessing from the Lord, when it is unrestrained and not governed by the boundaries He established in His Word, then it becomes a bad thing with negative consequences. The Bible has numerous words of warning about the dangers and consequences of sexual acts outside of heterosexual marriage, more than I can address in the space of this chapter.

Incest, adultery, bestiality, homosexuality, prostitution, and fornication are all condemned in the Scriptures (Lev. 18; 1 Cor. 6:9–11, 15–17). If these acts were
not enough, the Bible offers the generic "sexual immorality" that serves as a catch-all category for matters
that extend outside of the marriage of a wife and husband. Paul exhorts his readers to "flee from sexual
immorality," noting that one who commits such sin does
so against his own body (1 Cor. 6:18). It is because of
"sexual immorality, impurity, passion, evil desire, and
covetousness" that "the wrath of God is coming" (Col.
3:5–6). Throughout the book of Revelation, sexual immorality is mentioned numerous times in relation to the
judgment of God. Again, while sin is sin, it seems that
this one (among others listed) moves God in a particular
manner (Rev. 2:14, 20–21; 9:21; 14:8; 17:2, 4; 18:3, 9).

Even if the physical acts never occur, the Lord is concerned about the matters of the heart. His concern is so
significant that He told us that it would be better for us
to rip out our eyes or cut off our hands, if such members
of our bodies led us to sin (Matt. 5:29–30). For even if we
never enter into the realm of action, for us to look with
"lustful intent" is the act of committing adultery in our
hearts (Matt. 5:27–28).

Internal and External Pressure

If the influence of pornography is as strong within the
church as some have claimed it to be, then not only is
this a major problem that must be addressed in relation
to one's daily walk with the Lord, but it will hinder many
from taking the gospel to the nations. The quenching of
the Spirit of mission is the worst thing a believer can
do if he or she is to be on mission. Walking in habitual
disobedience to the Lord, as a result of the multitude of
sexual temptations from the global pornography industry, will greatly interfere with His work. Men and women

walking in such disobedience now are not likely to stop simply by going to another cultural context to tell people about Jesus. The temptations are there as well, and in some cases, are even more prevalent.

The stress of the field and spiritual warfare that comes from being on the frontline of kingdom advancement will only lead the believer into a heightened state of temptation. Therefore, if he or she does not confess, repent, and deal with this matter, then it is highly likely that massive problems will arise later when serving in the trenches.

However, the good news is that there is healing and restoration in Christ, especially for His children. I trained a church planter who applied to serve with a mission agency. During his interview, he revealed that he had occasionally looked at pornography over the previous year. While I was not aware of this matter, the agency rightly decided to assist this brother with his struggle and refrained from appointing him for service. They established a plan for him to receive some accountability and counsel with his local church for the next several months. After the agreed-upon time had passed and he had shown growth in this area, the agency agreed to interview him again. He later departed to serve and has been on the field to this day.

The external pressure on the church of the pornification of societies abound. Therefore, as unbelievers come into the kingdom, the church is going to have to care for, teach, and equip those who are likely to come with much history in the world of pornography. The effects of the consumption of such material will have affected the way the person thinks about manhood, womanhood, and sex—and the way that person lives as a sexual being created in the image of God. Grace, patience, and humility will be necessary in assisting new brothers and sisters as they move beyond the wickedness of the age.

Questions to Consider

1. Do you think that the pornification of societies is a pressure point on the church today? If so, why? If not, why not?

2. Do you struggle with pornography? If so, what are you actively doing to avoid it and rest in the grace of Christ in your life?

3. How can your church be proactive when it comes to addressing the problem of pornography today?

4. What can your church do to assist men and women with the struggles they may have with sexual sins?

Conclusion

Global Engagement in a World of Pressure Points

As we conclude this book, I would like to draw our attentions to a few matters related to our mission in this world that we are to carry out until Jesus returns. In a world filled with pressure points, how do we move forward in the beautiful assignment of making disciples of all nations? With the challenges of the age swirling around us, how do we move forward as followers of Jesus?

Understand the Pressure Points

As I mentioned at the beginning of this book, I have written this work to provide you with a big picture of twelve global realities that I believe are some of the most critical issues shaping the face of the church and mission both today and likely for the rest of our lives. Other global points of pressure exist, as well as local points of pressure unique to specific contexts. What I hope you understand is that you need to know the contexts in which you are serving and sending others to serve.

Numerous resources are available, written from both Christian and non-Christian perspectives on each of the twelve topics that I have addressed in this book. Take time to go deeper to better understand these matters and how best to minister in light of their realities. Listen to those in the trenches addressing how they are making disciples and planting churches in the slums, suburban, and inner-city contexts. Learn what is working to best advance the gospel in communities where poverty and HIV rates run high. Find out how to reach the unengaged Tangshuri of Afghanistan or Saaroa of Taiwan. Learn to think missiologically about the world around you so you may make wise practices on the field.

Know Your Box in View of the Pressure Points

We often hear the phrase "Think outside of the box," which is a call to consider possibilities other than what we are presently doing. While I am a strong advocate for such thinking and acting in light of the pressures around us, we must recognize that before we can consider other options, we must do an internal assessment. Dan Pallotta has written a helpful post for the *Harvard Business Review* titled, "Stop Thinking Outside of the Box."[1] In this blog post, he challenges his readers to understand the present organization where they find themselves in order to innovate and move beyond their limitations to health and growth. Consider his words: "You cannot possibly think outside the box unless you understand the nature of the box that bounds your current thinking. You must come to know that nature deeply. You must have real insight into it. You must accept it, and embrace it at some level, before it will ever release you." Though Pallotta's exhortation is written to the business world, it is helpful to us as well. We need to ask ourselves how well we understand our present circumstances within our churches, agencies, and institutions from a biblical and missiological perspective.

Some of us understand our situations very well. Some of us have very poor understandings. Kingdom stewardship involves ongoing evaluation of our present realities. We must resist the gravity that pulls us away from such reflection and take time to pray and think about such matters. It is my hope that this book has prompted you to consider your present situation and

Christ's commission in light of the pressure points surrounding us.

We should never make changes for the sake of change.
Spirit-led innovation involves us knowing our present
theological, missiological, philosphical, organizational,
and structural realities. We do not do new things for the
sake of doing something different or to appear hip or cut-
ting-edge. As the Spirit leads us in conjunction with the
wisdom He has provided in light of our present global
realities, we make adjustments for the building up of
the body of Christ. The Spirit is dynamic, so we should
not be surprised when He leads us to make changes. If
anything, we should be surprised at our resistance to
change.

We must understand the box in which we presently
find ourselves in order to make the necessary shifts
for gospel advancement and church multiplication.
Of course this reality will differ from denomination to
denomination, country to country, church to church,
and individual to individual. How well do you understand your present box? What are you doing to facilitate
the multiplication of disciples, leaders, and churches?
What is hindering the facilitation of the multiplication
of disciples, leaders, and churches? What must stay?
What must change?

Recognize Internal Pressures

In order to best understand our lives and churches, we
need to ask the Lord to open our eyes to sins that we need
to forsake, structures and organizations that we need to
change, and a vision for the nations that we need to embrace in light of the global pressure points. For many of
us, this will not be a pleasant experience, but remember that our Lord is abundantly gracious and amazingly
loving. His compassion for us is incredible. He died the
death we deserved to die and gave us the life that we

could not live (2 Cor. 5:21). We may come to see that materialism and its comforts are withholding us from making disciples of all nations. The sin of fear may be brought to our attentions as we consider what it means to advance the gospel in a world filled with pressure points. We may begin to recognize that our cherished programs, budgets, and organizations are actually hindering the rapid dissemination of the gospel and the multiplication of churches. The King and His ethic calls us to die to self and follow Him into a world filled with pressure (Luke 9:23–25). His call to become fishers of men and follow Him (Mark 1:17) is a call without consideration for our dreams, passions, and comforts.

Apart from us being continually filled with the Spirit of mission (Eph. 5:18), we will be overcome by the pressures of the age. For even as we walk in the Spirit, we should expect to be afflicted in every way, perplexed, persecuted, and struck down. Yet in light of these matters arising from faithfully serving Jesus in a world filled with pressure points, we are never crushed, driven to despair, forsaken, or destroyed (2 Cor. 4:8–9). Jesus reminded His disciples that they would have tribulations in the world, but He has overcome the world (John 16:29–33). And while tribulations do not automatically come with the pressure points of this world, it is crucial to know that He is greater than any of these overwhelming realities we experience today as we follow Him into the world. Apart from Him we can do nothing (John 15:5) and will cower in fear and refrain from taking the gospel to the nations.

Develop a Missionary Strategy

Assuming that a vision for glorifying God by making disciples of all nations has been obtained, healthy strategy needs to be developed in light of the pressures surrounding us. God is sovereign, but He expects

His church to be intentional, wise, and in accordance with His will. Our strategic planning is a prayerfully discerned, Spirit-guided process of preparation, development, implementation, and evaluation of the necessary steps involved for global disciple making.[2] This process can be developed by:

- asking good questions,
- responding with healthy answers,
- applying wise action steps,
- evaluating everything, and
- praying with diligence.

Use Wise Stewardship

With over four billion people in the world without Jesus, it is not wise to develop strategies that support methods which are counterproductive to the healthy rapid multiplication of disciples, leaders, and churches. Just because there is much biblical freedom in our culturally shaped methods does not mean that all such expressions are conducive to the multiplication of healthy churches across a people group or population segment.

Avoid Instant Gratification

We live in an instant society. We want results, and we want them now. This unhealthy philosophy has been in the church for the longest time, and our disciple-making and church-multiplication strategies are not immune to this plague. The pressure points around us help facilitate a move toward instant gratification due to the challenges they pose. Often our strategies are designed to bring instant gratification, thus allowing us to win the sprint of seeing numbers produced but failing the marathon of making disciples.

Hoist the Sails

The multiplication of disciples, leaders, and churches will only happen in relation to the sovereignty of God. The church cannot create movement. It is an act of the Spirit. We cannot program it. It is not achieved in four or five easy steps. However, we can hoist the sails on our boats so that if the Spirit does decide to move, He would be able to guide us in the direction of His will for the moment. An Old Testament story should give us reason to pause: the Lord desired His people to enter the Promised Land, and enter they did—forty years later. Our Father's will certainly will be done in the world, but will our generation be the means by which His Spirit may move to multiply disciples, leaders, and churches? Will our church be involved in that process, or are our actions hindering such a tremendous process? I can't say with certainty that we will be the means the Lord uses, but I can say that I do not believe the majority of our strategies are positioning us for a Spirit-led movement.

Keep It Simple

Complexity gives birth to complexity, and complexity is difficult to reproduce. Throughout the Bible we see a complex God empowering and working through simple, ordinary people to bring about extraordinary results. He works through the simple to bring glory to Himself (2 Cor. 4:7). Complexity is in creation, the Trinity, the Atonement, regeneration, and the mystery of Christ in you. Complexity is not a part of the means by which disciples are made and multiplied across the world. Whenever we examine the New Testament, we see that disciples were made and churches were birthed with little more than Spirit-filled sowers sharing the seed and allowing the Spirit to work (Acts 13–14; 1 Thess. 1:1–10).

The greater the complexity of our strategies and methods, the less likely we will experience multiplication.

Such involves an inverse relationship. As the diagram below portrays, everything we do is reproducible to some degree, but the question is, How reproducible is what we model before the people, reproducible by the people? The more technical our methods and strategies (falling closer to the left side of the diagram), the less likely the people we reach are going to be able to use those same approaches to reach those within their social networks.

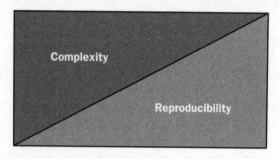

Reproducibility-Potential Guide[3]

The question we should ask is, "How reproducible is what we have modeled before the new believers reproducible by them?" We want the new believers to take the gospel message and spread it widely across their communities. We should strive to use missionary methods that are closer to the right side of the diagram, being more reproducible in our given context. If we tell the new church to imitate us as we imitate Christ (1 Cor. 11:1), how much of what we have modeled before them in both belief and practice is reproducible by them when it comes to planting other churches? When we teach them how to study the Bible, we keep the process simple. When we teach them how to pray, we keep it simple. When we teach them how to share their faith, we keep it simple. Why? Because the things of the Lord are not complicated, and the new believers are children in the faith. Jesus did the complicated part. Now the literate and illiterate, rich and poor, sick and healthy, urban and rural, educated and uneducated can serve Him faithfully in His church.

If we model a form of leadership before the people that only the few can imitate, then the possibility of multiplication will be diminished. For example, say I am a high-caliber leader, a ten-talented guy, a one-in-a-million guide, but I do not model a form of leadership before my people that those called out can imitate. Am I truly a good leader who is concerned with multiplication? Yes, there is a time and place to lead like a ten-talented leader. But, if my regular leadership style and ways of doing ministry are so lofty that they impress upon the people, "You can never serve the Lord like this—the way ministry should be done. I'll do everything for you. And only those of such a caliber as myself can be trusted with any significant ministry," then I am not a leader with the multiplication of disciples, leaders, and churches in mind. As we labor to keep things simple in the midst of complex pressure points, we should evaluate our methods in how well they:

1. communicate the gospel, the basic New Testament understanding of the local church, and what it means to obey all that Christ commanded;

2. facilitate the multiplication of healthy disciples and pastors and leaders in general; and

3. keep everything radically biblical and, thus, contextually simple in light of local pressure points.

Share Today's Stories Later Today

Among evangelicals in the 1980s and 1990s living in the United States, an atmosphere of pragmatism had developed. Many church leaders desiring growth in their churches were running from conference to conference and book to book, saying, "Tell me what works to grow the church." One of several limitations of this pragmatism was that it continued to foster the notion that nothing can be learned from others until they are able to provide the desired results. While we are to be pragmatic to a degree—we have been told to bear fruit and make disciples—an anything-goes philosophy, or one that only wants to listen to others whenever they have produced an outcome, is most unhealthy.

While at the Smithsonian National Air and Space Museum in Washington, my family and I once observed a fascinating historic relic, the Bell X-1. This was the first plane to break the sound barrier. Chuck Yeager surpassed the Mach 1 speed in October 1947, and he will always be remembered as the first man to accomplish this great task.

For years, many people believed that the sound barrier could not be broken. Numerous attempts were made, many aircraft broke apart, countless hours were spent, and enormous costs were paid that finally resulted in the accomplishment of the desired goal. The scientists, engineers, and test pilots needed all of these stories of failure before they could tell Yeager's story. But we don't hear or remember the stories that preceded Yeager. We want the results.

We like to share the stories that reveal the thrill of victory, but we often fail to tell those that remember the agony of defeat. We create a culture that is opposed to hearing the unsuccessful stories, fooling ourselves into believing that such is a practice of wise stewards. Ironically, the unsuccessful stories are often successful when measured by the kingdom standard.

Whenever we do share, we often take a long time before we tell our stories. For example, a church planter arrives on the field, uses a multitude of methods, finds some that work, and writes a book telling what resulted in the planting of the church. Or, consider another example. A pastor works for years, trying to reach people with the gospel, teach them the ways of Jesus, and raise them up to become missionaries. He tries many things over the years; most of them do not work so well.

Finally, he compiles all that has worked and hits the speaking circuit, sharing what has been effective—and eventually writing down his story of success.

The time spent between the date we hit the field and the date we begin telling our stories is too long. We must compress time. We start telling our stories too late in the game. By the time we begin to share with others what worked, society and the contextual realities have often shifted. Of course, the church hears such wonderful accounts and immediately begins to apply what was learned, often five to fifteen years after the fact. Don't wait around to break the sound barrier before you start sharing. That is likely to take too much time. We need to know why your jet is shaped like a .50 caliber bullet. Why are you using super-thin wings and an adjustable horizontal stabilizer? We need to know why your last attempt resulted in the pilot ejecting before a crash. We need to know why you decided to change your fuel mixture. We need to know why you decided that it was best to attempt such a feat over the Mojave Desert. And we need to know these details as soon as possible. Rather than waiting years to tell one side of your story of reaching the nations, will you compress time to advance the gospel? We need to learn from each other today.

The global pressure points are too widespread and too great for us to spend years attempting to make disciples of all nations and only share our stories of great and glorious results years after such outcomes occur. We must remember that as we are faithful, God's glory is evident in the struggles for gospel advancement. Churches are not in competition with one another. We are not like corporations that spend millions of dollars on top secret research and development departments, running test after test until years later, when we finally get the perfect product, we can roll it out to the public for sale.

We must begin to communicate our stories now—both what is working well and what is not working so well. It is wise and healthy to say, "We don't know the answer, but here is what we have tried." If someone is only one step ahead of someone else in the process of making disciples, then that person has at least one thing to teach those who follow. Sometimes he can teach them what to do; sometimes she can teach them what to avoid. But they can teach something.

This does not mean that you have to share great details, but tell us something. And tell us now. We need to learn from you. As wise stewards, we cannot wait around, thinking that maybe we'll have something to share tomorrow. Today is the day for sharing! Start talking. Start blogging. Start tweeting. Start publishing. Get your experiences out there!

Our Father is always at work; we need to realize this fact and stop giving glory to God only when He does what we desire. He is worthy of glory even when He chooses not to fulfill our strategies.

Remain Grounded in the Word of the Ages

When the Son of Man returns, will He find us faithful? Many of the pressure points of the age could easily push us from our biblical moorings. The challenges arising from the pressures of our time are so great that we could easily follow the path of fear, paralysis, fatigue, apathy, or complacency. Our only hope is to avoid such detours by following the Way. We must remember that He has overcome the world (John 16:33) and, by His grace, so have we (1 John 5:4). Being born of God, we are more than conquerors of the challenges of the age that try to separate us from the love of Christ (Rom 8:37). As we remain in the Word, walking in the light as He is in the light, His leadership will keep us on the right path. Apart from abiding in Him, all of our strategies, methods, desires, and interests are worthless for the sake of the kingdom. Greater is He who is in us than are the pressure points in the world.

Acknowledgments

Though a book bears the name of an author, you are reading this right now because of the commitment of many people. And while I take full credit for the shortcomings found in this work, I must say thank you to several of those who kept those shortcomings to a minimum. This is my second book with Thomas Nelson. All of the brothers and sisters there have been of great assistance on this book. I worked with two editors on this project. I began with Heather McMurray and finished with Maleah Bell. Both of these ladies and their teams are to be commended for their work on this project.

While writing this book, I experienced a significant transition in my life. After serving ten years as a professor and missionary with the Southern Baptist Theological Seminary and North American Mission Board, the Lord called me to The Church at Brook Hills in Birmingham, Alabama, where I serve as the pastor of church multiplication. Before the transition, Matt Pierce, my research assistant, and Amber Walsh, my secretary, both assisted me with some of the research behind this book. Thank you both for your commitment and friendship. It was a delight to serve with you.

I am writing these acknowledgements seven months after arriving in Birmingham. Over these months, the grace of the Lord has been shown tremendously through my new faith family. I have the delight to serve alongside of a Spirit-filled staff and elders. I am also very thankful for the friendship and the pastoral staff of John, Jim, David, Jonathan, Keith, Donnie, Matt, and Dennis. You guys are wonderful kindred spirits with whom it is a delight to lock arms in the journey. Thank you, faith family, for your understanding, prayers, and words of encouragement for my family and me since we arrived.

You have greatly assisted me in the completion of this book. It is a tremendous honor to be one of your pastors and to co-labor with you as we work to make disciples of all nations.

Of course, I cannot fail to say thank you to four very special people in the Payne house: Sarah, Hannah, Rachel, and Joel. Your love, presence, words of encouragement, and prayers have been greatly needed throughout this writing project. Thank you so much. And, Sarah, thank you for supporting me and patiently encouraging me on this book in light of our recent transition and all the points of pressure that came with it as well. I think you are an amazing woman of God, and I am deeply honored to be called your husband.

Notes

Chapter 1

1. David A. Fraser, "The 2.4 Billion: Why Are We Still so Unconcerned?" in *Perspectives on the World Christian Movement: A Reader*, Ralph D. Winter and Steven C. Hawthorne, eds., rev. ed. (Pasadena, CA: William Carey Library, 1992), 191.

2. "Turkey: World's Largest Unreached People Group?" (October 21, 2011), *Mission Network News*, accessed January 20, 2013, http://mnnonline.org/article/16374.

3. Ralph D. Winter, "3 Men, 3 Eras," *Mission Frontiers* 3, no. 2 (February 1981): 7.

4. Lausanne Occasional Papers, "Ministry Among Least Reached People Groups," (2005), 8, accessed December 21, 2012, http://www.lausanne.org/en/documents/lops/848–lop-35a.html.

5. Ibid., 19.

6. "World Christian Database," accessed March 18, 2013, http://www.worldchristiandatabase.org/wcd/.

7. "Joshua Project," accessed March 18, 2013, http://www.joshuaproject.net/index.php.

8. "Global Research: IMB Connecting," accessed March 18, 2013, http://public.imb.org/globalresearch/Pages/default.aspx.

9. Ibid.

10. According to the Global Research Department of the International Mission Board,

   An Evangelical Christian is a person who believes that Jesus Christ is the sole source of salvation through faith in Him, has personal faith and conversion with regeneration by the Holy Spirit, recognizes the inspired Word of God as the only basis for faith and Christian living, and is committed to biblical preaching and evangelism that brings others to faith in Jesus Christ.

175

Therefore, an Evangelical church is a church that is characterized by these same beliefs and principles.

"Frequently Asked Questions," Global Research: IMB Connecting, accessed December 21, 2012, http://public.imb.org/globalresearch/Pages/FAQs.aspx#seven.

11. Ralph D. Winter and Bruce A. Koch, "Finishing the Task," in Ralph D. Winter and Steven C. Hawthorne, eds., *Perspectives*, 4th ed. (Pasadena, CA: William Carey Library, 2009), 543.

12. Todd M. Johnson and Charles L. Tieszen, "Personal Contact: The *sine qua non* of Twenty-first Century Christian Mission," *Evangelical Missions Quarterly* 43, no. 4 (October 2007): 494–502.

13. David B. Barrett and Todd M. Johnson, *World Christian Trends AD 30–AD 2200: Interpreting the Annual Christian Megacensus* (Pasadena, CA: William Carey Library, 2001), 656.

Chapter 2

1. George G. Hunter III, *How to Reach Secular People* (Nashville, TN: Abingdon Press, 1992), 37.

2. Though the Western world is certainly larger than the United States, due to my experience and place of residence, I am writing much of this chapter with my country in mind.

3. Lesslie Newbigin, *The Gospel in a Pluralist Society* (Grand Rapids, MI: William B. Eerdmans; Geneva: WCC Publications, 1989), 242.

4. Barna Group, "Most Americans Are Concerned about Restrictions in Religious Freedom," January 18, 2013, accessed March 18, 2013, http://www.barna.org/culture-articles/600–most-americans-are-concerned-about-restrictions-in-religious-freedom.

5. Lesslie Newbigin, *Foolishness to the Greeks: The Gospel and Western Culture* (Grand Rapids, MI: William B. Eerdmans, 1986), 3.

6. "'Nones' on the Rise: One-in-Five Adults Have No Religious Affiliation," Pew Forum on Religion and Public Life, October 9, 2012, accessed March 18, 2013, http://www.pewforum.org/Unaffiliated/nones-on-the-rise-religion.aspx.

7. "U.S. Religious Landscape Survey," Pew Forum on Religion and Public Life, accessed December 20, 2012, http://religions.pewforum.org/affiliations.

8. Jason Mandryk, *Operation World: The Definitive Prayer Guide to Every Nation*, 7th ed. (Colorado Springs: Biblica, 2010), 118, 194, 341, 360, 624, 632, 765, 800, 854.

9. "Evangelical Protestant States (2010)," Association of Religion Data Archives, accessed January 20, 2013, http://thearda.com/ql2010/QL_S_2010_1_27p.asp.

10. "Evangelical Protestant Metro Areas (2010)," Association of Religion Data Archives, accessed January 8, 2013, http://www.thearda.com/ql2010/QL_M_2010_1_27c.asp; J. D. Payne, "Least Reached Metro Areas in the U.S.," *Missiologically Thinking* (blog), June 11, 2012, http://www.jdpayne.org/2012/06/11/least-reached-metro-areas-in-the-u-s/.

11. "'Nones' on the Rise," 9, 13.

12. "Faith on the Move: The Religious Affiliation of International Migrants," Pew Forum on Religion and Public Life, March 8, 2012, accessed March 18, 2013, http://www.pewforum.org/Geography/Religious-Migration-exec.aspx, 11.

13. Ibid., 16–17.

14. When I use the adjective *apostolic*, I am not referring to a denomination or a church. I am not referring to someone who is like the Twelve and communicates extrabiblical revelation on par with the Scriptures. I am simply using a derivative of the New Testament Greek word that I believe better communicates the New Testament truth of the nature of those whom churches send with the message of the gospel to plant churches. I prefer this word to the Latin translation of *mitto* from which we derive *missionary* with all of its historical and contemporary connotations.

Chapter 3

1. While Catholicism already had a presence in the Philippines for centuries, Protestant missionaries arrived in the late nineteenth century. Charles has written several books, including the excellent *Indigenous Church Planting: A Practical Journey* (Neosho, MO: Church Growth International, 1990). Learn more about his work at http://www.churchgrowthinternational.com.

2. The term *Majority World* has been accepted in missiological circles as an appropriate way (among others) to describe the traditionally non-Western countries without prejudice or stereotype. *Majority* is simply a demographic designation noting that the majority of the world's population resides in such countries.

3. Jason Mandryk, *Operation World: The Definitive Prayer Guide to Every Nation*, 7th ed. (Colorado Springs: Biblica, 2010), 642.

4. "Private Jets for Jesus," *Christianity Today Online*, December 10, 2102, accessed March 19, 2013, http://www.christianitytoday. com/ct/2012/december-web-only/private-jets-for-jesus.html?utm_ source=ctdirect-html&utm_medium=Newsletter&utm_ term=11656672&utm_content=145394824&utm_ campaign=2012.

5. Mandryk, 642, 643.

6. Ibid., 510.

7. Mark A. Noll, *The New Shape of World Christianity: How American Experience Reflects Global Faith* (Downers Grove, IL: IVP, 2009), 20–21.

8. Philip Jenkins, *The Next Christendom: The Coming of Global Christianity* (New York: Oxford University, 2002), 3.

9. "U.S. Religious Landscape Survey," Pew Forum on Religion and Public Life, accessed December 10, 2012, http://religions. pewforum.org/maps; Mandryk, 914 lists the United States as 29 percent evangelical.

10. Mandryk, 914.

11. Mandryk, 950, 951. In the original source, China, PRC, was listed as sending 100,000 missionaries. In an e-mail correspondence with Mandryk when writing my book, *Strangers Next Door: Immigration, Migration, and Mission*, I was informed that 20,000 is a more accurate number for China. Also, the numbers in this table are limited to missionaries serving longer than two years; represent Protestant, Independent, and Anglican missionaries; and are not limited to international workers. These numbers also do not reflect many of the believers evangelizing or church-planting in diaspora, or those missionary movements that are decentralized and not monitored by churches.

12. Edwin Zehner, "One-Way Missions in the Age of Global Christianity: A View from Thailand," *International Journal of Frontier Missiology* 27, no. 2 (Summer 2010): 80.

13. Adam Miller, "In Norwich Connecting," *On Mission*, accessed December 12, 2012, http://www.onmission.com/In_Norwich_connecting/.

14. Jehu J. Hanciles, *Beyond Christendom: Globalization, African Migration, and the Transformation of the West* (New York, NY: Orbis Books, 2008), 344.

Chapter 4

1. Gail Russell Chaddok, "Inauguration Day Bibles: How Presidents Choose, and What that Reveals," *Christian Science Monitor*, January 21, 2013, http://www.csmonitor.com/USA/DC-Decoder/2013/0121/Inauguration-Day-Bibles-how-presidents-choose-and-what-that-reveals-video.

2. Brendan O'Brien, "Wisconsin Sikh Temple Gunman Killed Himself: FBI," *Reuters*, August 8, 2012, accessed March 19, 2013, http://www.reuters.com/article/2012/08/08/us-usa-shooting-shooter-idUSBRE8770X720120808.

3. Islam is also an exclusive faith tradition. While it would agree with the pluralistic mind-set of much of the Western world that Jesus is not the only way, it would disagree for extremely different reasons.

4. Pew Forum on Religion and Public Life, "The Global Religious Landscape: A Report on the Size and Distribution of the World's Major Religious Groups as of 2010," accessed March 19, 2013, http://www.pewforum.org/global-religious-landscape-exec.aspx, 29, 32, 35, 39.

5. "Fast Facts on the Baha'i Faith," Religion Facts, accessed January 11, 2013, http://www.religionfacts.com/bahai/fast_facts.htm.

6. Pew Forum on Religion and Public Life, "The Future of the Global Muslim Population: Projections for 2010–2030," accessed March 19, 2013, http://www.pewforum.org/the-future-of-the-global-muslim-population.aspx, 11, 13, 15, 19, 20.

7. Ibid. In December 2012, Pew Research Center published "The Global Religious Landscape: A Report on the Size and Distribution of the World's Major Religious Groups as of 2010"; the information on the top ten countries with the largest Muslim populations for 2010 are slightly different estimations than those in their 2011 publication.

8. Pew, "Future of Muslim Population," 15, 19, 121.

9. Patrick Johnstone, *The Future of the Global Church: History, Trends, and Possibilities* (Colorado Springs: Biblica, 2011), 78.

10. "'Nones' on the Rise: One-in-Five Adults Have No Religious Affiliation," Pew Forum on Religion and Public Life, October 9, 2012, accessed March 18, 2013, http://www.pewforum.org/Unaffiliated/nones-on-the-rise-religion.aspx.

11. Pew, "Global Religious Landscape," 25.

Chapter 5

1. Sharon Mager, "Five hundred come to Christ and two churches start as a result of Nepal/India mission trip," *Baptist Life*, accessed August 17, 2009, http://www.baptistlifeonline.org/2009/08/five-hundred-come-to-christ-and-two-churches-start-as-a-result-of-nepalindia-mission-trip.

2. Stephen Castles and Mark J. Miller, *The Age of Migration: International Population Movements in the Modern World*, 4th ed. (New York: Gilford, 2009).

3. W. M. Spellman, *The Global Community: Migration and the Making of the Modern World* (London: Sutton, 2002), 74–75.

4. Oscar Handlin, *The Uprooted: The Epic Story of the Great Migrations That Made the American People*, 2nd ed. (Boston: Little Brown and Co., 1979), 32–33.

5. Jeremy Hein, "France: The Melting Pot of Europe," in *Migration and Immigration: A Global View*, ed. Maura I. Toro-Morn and Marixsa Alicea (Westport, CT: Greenwood, 2004), 72.

6. United Nations, Department of Economic and Social Affairs, "Trends in the International Migrant Stock: The 2008 Revision," accessed February 15, 2011, http://www.un.org/esa/population/migration/UN_MigStock_2008.pdf.

7. United Nations, "International Migrant Stock: The 2008 Revision," accessed February 15, 2011, http://esa.un.org/migration/index.asp?panel=1.

8. Home Office Statistical Bulletin, "British Citizenship Statistics United Kingdom, 2008," May 20, 2009, accessed January 25, 2011, http://rds.homeoffice.gov.uk/rds/pdfs09/hosb0909.pdf.

9. Alain Bélanger and Éric Caron Malenfant, "Ethnocultural Diversity in Canada: Prospects for 2017," Canadian Social Trends (Winter 2005), 19, accessed February 28, 2013, http://www5.statcan.gc.ca/

access_acces/alternative_alternatif.action?l=eng&loc=http://www. statcan.gc.ca/pub/11-008-x/2005003/article/8968-eng.pdf&t= Ethnocultural%20diversity%20in%20Canada:%20Prospects%20 for%202017.

10. United Nations, "International Migrant Stock."

11. J. D. Payne, *Strangers Next Door: Immigration, Migration, and Mission* (Downers Grove, IL: InterVarsity Press, 2012), 361.

12. Conor Dougherty and Miriam Jordan, "Minority Births Are New Majority," *Wall Street Journal*, May 17, 2012, accessed January 25, 2013, http://online.wsj.com/article/SB100014240527023038 79604577408363003351818.html.

13. United States Census Bureau, "U.S. Census Bureau Projections Show a Slower Growing, Older, More Diverse Nation a Half Century from Now," accessed January 25, 2013, http://www. census.gov/newsroom/releases/archives/population/cb12–243. html.

14. United States Census Bureau, "The Foreign-Born Population in the United States: 2010" (May 2012), accessed January 25, 2013, http://www.census.gov/prod/2012pubs/acs-19.pdf.

15. Institute of International Education, "Open Doors Data: International Students; Leading Places of Origin," accessed December 13, 2012, http://www.iie.org/Research-and-Publications/Open-Doors/ Data/International-Students/Leading-Places-of-Origin/2010-12.

16. Institute of International Education, "Project Atlas: France," accessed December 13, 2012, http://www.iie.org/Services/Project-Atlas/France.

17. Studies in Australia, "International Students in Australia," accessed December 13, 2012, http://www.studiesinaustralia.com/ studying-in-australia/why-study-in-australia/international-students-in-australia.

18. "Syrian Refugees to Receive 20,000 Family Hygiene Kits," United Nations Population Fund, accessed March 19, 2013, http:// www.unfpa.org/public/cache/offonce/home/news/pid/12640; jsessionid=8FE94E7910C7420E5F8E7DDD6F9DE6D9.jahia02.

19. Trey Mewes, "Destination Austin for Burmese Refugees," *Austin Daily Herald*, December 14, 2012, accessed March 19, 2013, http://www.austindailyherald.com/2012/12/14/destination-austin-for-burmese-refugees/.

20. Kwanele Sibanda, "Zambia: Congo Refugees Ordered to Leave," AfricaNews, May 1, 2009, accessed March 19, 2013, http://www.

africanews.com/site/Zambia_Congo_refugees_ordered_to_leave/list_messages/24602.

21. Tony Kushner and Katharine Knox, *Refugees in an Age of Genocide* (New York: Frank Cass, 1999).

22. "History of UNHCR," United Nations High Commissioner for Refugees, accessed January 23, 2011, http://www.unhcr.org/pages/49c3646cbc.html.

23. "Convention and Protocol Relating to the Status of Refugees," United Nations High Commissioner for Refugees, accessed January 23, 2011, http://www.unhcr.org/3b66c2aa10.html.

24. "Global Trends 2011," United Nations High Commissioner for Refugees, accessed December 14, 2012, http://www.unhcr.org/4fd6f87f9.html.

25. Lausanne Committee for World Evangelization, "Scattered to Gather: Embracing the Global Trend of Diaspora" (Manila: LifeChange, 2010). A copy of this booklet as a pdf may be downloaded from my blog http://www.jdpayne.org/wp-content/uploads/2010/10/Scattered-to-Gather.pdf and has been posted there with permission.

26. Payne, 150–158.

27. This story of Marietta is adapted from Lorajoy Tira Dimangon-dayao, "All to All People: Samples of Diaspora Filipinos Making Kingdom Impact," in *Scattered: The Filipino Global Presence*, ed. Luis Pantoja Jr., Sadiri Joy Tira, and Enoch Wan (Manila: LifeChange, 2004), 302.

Chapter 6

1. Richard M. Sherman, Robert B. Sherman, "It's a Small World (After All)," (Burbank: Wonderland, 1963).

2. Manfred B. Steger, *Globalization: A Very Short Introduction*, American ed. (New York: Oxford University Press, 2009), 36.

3. George Ritzer, *Globalization: The Essentials* (London: Wiley and Sons, 2011), 3–17.

4. Justin Harper, "Airline Boom Leaves Asia Short of Pilots," *Telegraph*, December 5, 2011, accessed January 28, 2013, http://www.telegraph.co.uk/finance/personalfinance/expat-money/8935358/Airline-boom-leaves-Asia-short-of-pilots.html.

5. William Voss, quoted in Harper, "Airline Boom."

6. International Telecommunication Union, *Measuring the Information Society 2012*, Executive Summary (Geneva, Switzerland, International Telecommunication Union, 2012), 1–3, accessed January 3, 2013, http://www.itu.int/ITU-D/ict/publications/idi/index.html.

7. Miriam Adeney, "Is God Colorblind or Colorful? The Gospel, Globalization, and Ethnicity," in *One World or Many? The Impact of Globalization on Mission*, Richard Tiplady, ed. (Pasadena, CA: William Carey Library, 2003), 99.

Chapter 7

1. "World Bank Sees Progress Against Extreme Poverty, But Flags Vulnerabilities," World Bank, February 29, 2012, accessed September 14, 2012, http://web.worldbank.org/WBSITE/EXTERNAL/NEWS/0,,contentMDK:23130032~pagePK:64257043~piPK:437376~theSitePK:4607,00.html.

2. Frank Rijsberman, "Waiting for a Solution," *Urban World* 4, no. 4 (December 2011): 10–11, accessed November 20, 2012, http://www.unhabitat.org/pmss/listItemDetails.aspx?publicationID=3263.

3. United Nations, *The State of Food Insecurity in the World* (Rome: Food and Agriculture Organization of the United Nations, 2012), 8, 11.

4. Paul Borthwick, *Western Christians in Global Mission: What's the Role of the North American Church* (Downers Grove, IL: InterVarsity, 2012), 79–80.

5. Steve Corbett and Brian Fikkert, *When Helping Hurts: How to Alleviate Poverty Without Hurting the Poor . . . and Yourself* (Chicago: Moody, 2009), 104.

6. Donald A. McGavran, *Understanding Church Growth*, ed. C. Peter Wagner, 3rd ed. (Grand Rapids: Eerdmans, 1970), 209.

Chapter 8

1. UN Habitat, *State of the World's Cities 2010/2011: Bridging the Urban Divide* (London: Earthscan, 2008), 5.

2. J. John Palen, *The Urban World*, 6th ed. (Boston, MA: McGraw Hill, 2002), 9.

3. Ibid., 7.

4. UNICEF, "Children in an Urban World: The State of the World's Children 2012, Executive Summary," 12–13, accessed March 20, 2013, http://www.unicef.org/sowc2012/.

5. John J. Macionis and Vincent N. Parrillo, *Cities and Urban Life* (Upper Saddle River, New Jersey: Prentice-Hall, 1998), 41.

6. United Nations Department of Economic and Social Affairs, "World Urbanization Prospects: The 2011 Revision" (New York: United Nations, 2012), 1, 3–6, 12–13.

7. *Atlas of Global Development*, 3rd ed. (Glasgow: Collins; Washington: World Bank, 2011), 28–29.

8. Robert Neuwirth, *Shadow Cities: A Billion Squatters, A New Urban World* (London: Routledge, 2008), xiii.

9. United Nations, "World Urbanization," 11.

10. Ibid., 7.

11. Paul G. Hiebert and Eloise Hiebert Meneses, *Incarnational Ministry: Planting Churches in Band, Tribal, Peasant, and Urban Societies* (Grand Rapids, MI: Baker Books, 1995), 271.

12. UN Habitat, *State of the World's Cities*, xii.

13. Neuwirth, *Shadow Cities*, xiii.

14. UN Habitat, *State of the World's Cities*, 33.

15. Ibid., 32.

16. Ibid., 52.

17. United States Census Bureau, "Growth in Urban Population Outpaces Rest of the Nation, Census Bureau Reports," March 26, 2012, accessed January 29, 2013, http://www.census.gov/newsroom/releases/archives/2010_census/cb12–50.html.

Chapter 9

1. Population Reference Bureau, "2012 World Population Data Sheet," 10, accessed January 30, 2012, http://www.prb.org/Publications/Datasheets/2012/world-population-data-sheet/data-sheet.aspx.

2. United Nations, "Youth: Social Policy and Development Division," Department of Economic and Social Affairs, accessed January 31, 2013, http://social.un.org/index/Youth/FAQs.aspx.

3. Population Reference Bureau, "2012 World Population," 10.

4. United Nations, "Regional Overview: The State of Youth in Asia and the Pacific," accessed January 31, 2013, http://social.un.org/youthyear/docs/ESCAPFinal5.pdf.

5. United Nations, "Regional Overview: Youth in the Arab Region," accessed January 31, 2013, http://social.un.org/youthyear/docs/Regional%20Overview%20Youth%20in%20the%20Arab%20Region-Western%20Asia.pdf.

6. United Nations, "Regional Overview: Youth in Africa," accessed January 31, 2013, http://social.un.org/youthyear/docs/Regional%20Overview%20Youth%20in%20Africa.pdf.

7. United States Census Bureau, "State and Country QuickFacts: USA," accessed January 31, 2013, http://quickfacts.census.gov/qfd/states/00000.html.

8. United States Census Bureau, "U.S. Census Bureau Projections Show a Slower Growing, Older, More Diverse Nation a Half Century from Now," December 12, 2012, accessed January 31, 2013, http://www.census.gov/newsroom/releases/archives/population/cb12–243.html.

9. Hope Yen, "Census: Share of Children in US Hits Record Low," Associated Press, July 12, 2011, accessed January 31, 2013, http://news.yahoo.com/census-share-children-us-hits-record-low-192800740.html.

10. United States Census Bureau, "Facts for Features: Back to School: 2012–2013," July 24, 2012, accessed January 31, 2013, http://www.census.gov/newsroom/releases/archives/facts_for_features_special_editions/cb11–_ff15.html.

11. United Nations World Youth Report, "Youth Migration and Development," accessed December 27, 2012, www.unworldyouthreport.org.

12. UNICEF, "State of the World's Children 2012," 6, accessed December 28, 2012, http://www.unicef.org/sowc2012/.

13. M. A. Madrigal, quoted in Rob McBride, "Combating Child Sexual Exploitation in the Philippines Pornography Trade," UNICEF Media Centre, November 17, 2008, accessed March 24, 2013, http://www.unicef.org/eapro/media_9675.html.

14. UNICEF, "World's Children 2012," 2.

15. Ed Payne, "European Police Arrest 103 in Suspected Human Trafficking Ring," CNN International, January 31, 2013, accessed January 31, 2013, http://edition.cnn.com/2013/01/31/

world/europe/human-trafficking-arrests/index.html?sr=
sharebar_twitter.

16. United States Department of State, "Trafficking in Persons Report, June 2012," 33–34, accessed December 28, 2012, http://www.state.gov/j/tip/rls/tiprpt/2012/index.htm.

17. U.S. Department of State, "Victims' Stories," accessed March 24, 2013, http://www.state.gov/j/tip/rls/tiprpt/2011/164225.htm.

18. Ibid.

19. UNICEF, "World's Children 2012," 6.

20. United Nations, "Fact Sheet: Health of Young People," accessed January 31, 2013, http://social.un.org/youthyear/docs/who-youth-health.pdf.

21. United Nations, "Fact Sheet: HIV and Young People," accessed January 31, 2013, http://social.un.org/youthyear/docs/youth-hiv.pdf.

22. United Nations, "Youth in Africa."

23. UNICEF, "World's Children 2012," 4–5.

24. "Evangelism Is Most Effective among Kids," Barna Group, October 11, 2004, accessed December 27, 2012, http://www.barna.org/barna-update/article/5–barna-update/196–evangelism-is-most-effective-among-kids.

Chapter 10

1. "Measles Outbreak Kills Hundreds in Pakistan," *Al Jazeera*, January 2, 2013, http://www.aljazeera.com/news/asia/2013/01/20131282648859762.html.

2. Robert Herriman, "Peru's Amazonian Region Battle Dengue Fever Outbreak," *Global Dispatch*, January 1, 2013, accessed January 2, 2013, http://www.theglobaldispatch.com/perus-amazonian-region-battle-dengue-fever-outbreak-37414/.

3. United Nations Children's Fund, *Committing to Child Survival: A Promise Renewed, Progress Report 2012* (New York: UNICEF, 2012), 15.

4. *Atlas of Global Development*, 3rd ed. (Glasgow: Collins; Washington: World Bank, 2011), 59.

5. World Health Organization, "The 17 Neglected Tropical Diseases," accessed January 2, 2013, http://www.who.int/neglected_diseases/diseases/en/.

6. World Health Organization, *World Health Statistics 2012* (Geneva: WHO, 2012), 12–14, 16, 34–36.

7. United Nations Department of Economic and Social Affairs/ Population Division, *World Mortality Report 2011* (New York: United Nations, 2012), 3–4.

8. Ibid., 9.

9. Ibid.

10. Ibid., 10.

11. Ibid., 13.

12. Ibid., 4, 9.

13. Ibid., 12.

14. *Atlas of Global Development*, 49.

15. Ibid., 54.

16. Ibid., 58.

17. *UNAIDS Report on the Global AIDS Epidemic: 2012*, (Joint United Nations Programme on HIV/AIDS), 8, accessed March 24, 2013, http://www.unaids.org/en/media/unaids/contentassets/ documents/epidemiology/2012/gr2012/20121120_UNAIDS_ Global_Report_2012_en.pdf.

18. *Atlas of Global Development*, 58.

19. United Nations, *World Mortality*, 28–29.

20. *Atlas of Global Development*, 13.

21. Ibid., 108, 110.

22. John Piper, "One Life: Don't Waste It" (address, Campus Outreach National Conference, Chattanooga, TN, January 1, 2012), accessed January 31, 2013, http://www.youtube.com/ watch?v=UgQC_002430.

Chapter 11

1. International Orality Network, *Making Disciples of Oral Learners* (Hampden, MA: Elim, 2005), 3.

2. Tex Sample, *Ministry in an Oral Culture: Living with Will Rogers, Uncle Remus, and Minnie Pearl* (Louisville: Westminister/ John Knox Press, 1994), 6.

3. Walter J. Ong, *Orality and Literacy: The Technologizing of the World* (New York: Routledge, 1982), 7.

4. International Orality Network, 3.

5. Grant Lovejoy, "Not a Passing Fad," Lausanne Movement, November 2, 2010, accessed January 2, 2013, http://conversation. lausanne.org/en/conversations/detail/10044#.UOSHbPHPNyo.

6. International Orality Network, 79–90.

7. Grant I. Lovejoy, James B. Slack, and J. O. Terry, eds., *Chronological Bible Storying: A Methodology for Presenting the Gospel to Oral Communicators* (Fort Worth, TX: Southwestern Baptist Theological Seminary, 2001), I.21–I.22.

8. C. Peter Wagner, *Strategies for Church Growth: Tools for Effective Mission and Evangelism* (Ventura, CA: Regal Books, 1989), 91–92.

Chapter 12

1. I recognize that a chapter on pornography in a book on global pressures shaping the face of the church and mission may seem out of place. It was odd for me when I first considered it. In fact, this chapter was not in my original plan for this book. However, two months before my deadline, I felt compelled to include it after prayer and conversation with others from different walks of life. This was a surprising experience for me. Before writing a book, I outline the components and conduct my research. Making such a change—and a seemingly out-of-place one at that—is not normative. In fact, this is my eighth book as a single author, and never have I made such a revision before.

2. Interestingly, some have described hard-core pornography as the "crack cocaine" of today. Associated Press, "Addiction to Porn Destroying Lives, Senate Told: Experts Compare Effect on Brain to That of Heroin or Crack Cocaine," NBC News, November 19, 2004.

3. Patrick Wanis, "How Women Made Porn Fashionable," FoxNews.com, September 15, 2012, accessed January 15, 2013, http://www.foxnews.com/opinion/2012/09/15/how-women-made-porn-fashionable.

4. "Porn Profits: Corporate America's Secret," ABC News, January 28, 2013, accessed March 24, 2013, http://abcnews.go.com/Primetime/story?id=132001&page=1#.UU822xzvvjU.

5. Rebecca Leung, "Porn in the U.S.A.," CBS News, December 5, 2007, accessed January 15, 2013, http://www.cbsnews.com/8301-18560_162-585049.html.

6. Dan Ackman, "How Big Is Porn?" Forbes.com, May 5, 2001, accessed January 15, 2013, http://www.forbes.com/2001/05/25/0524porn.html.

7. Jerry Ropelato, "Internet Pornography Statistics," Top Ten Reviews, accessed January 26, 2013, http://internet-filter-review.toptenreviews.com/internet-pornography-statistics.html. It should also be noted that after writing this chapter, I discovered that the link to Ropelato's findings now does not list all of the numbers he originally included in a series of tables and graphs. What is now found at the link is a user-friendly visual portraying some of his findings. The original information, including what is cited in this chapter, is now archived at http://archive.is/I4qA (accessed March 4, 2013).

Just because many people—including scholars—reference a source does not mean that the source provides accurate information. Accurate statistics on pornography and personal sexual matters are not easy to obtain, especially on a global scale. Until more research is conducted and findings published, we have to rely on what is available while admitting the possible limitations to our research.

8. Ashlee Vance, "Online Porn is Huge. Like Really, Really Huge. Who Knew?" *Bloomberg Businessweek*, April 5, 2012, accessed January 15, 2013, http://www.businessweek.com/articles/2012-04-05/online-porn-is-huge-dot-like-really-really-huge-dot-who-knew.

9. Ted Thornhill, "Is the Whole World Looking at Porn? Biggest Site Gets Over Four Billion Hits a Month," Mail Online, April 9, 2012, accessed March 4, 2013, http://www.dailymail.co.uk/sciencetech/article-2127201/Porn-site-Xvideos-worlds-biggest-4bn-hits-month-30-web-traffic-porn.html.

10. Ropelato.

11. "The Stats on Internet Porn," Online MBA, June 18, 2010, accessed January 16, 2013, http://www.onlinemba.com/blog/the-stats-on-internet-porn.

12. Meredith Bennett-Smith, "Porn Now a 'Global Phenomenon' Increasingly Fueled by People Watching at Work: Report," *Huffington Post*, November 19, 2012, accessed January 15, 2013, http://www.huffingtonpost.com/2012/11/19/porn-global-phenomenon-fueled-people-work_n_2161509.html.

13. Ropelato.

14. Emma Graham-Harrison, "Afghanistan Cracks Down on Internet Cafes for Allowing Porn," October 25, 2010, accessed March 24, 2013, http://blogs.reuters.com/afghanistan/2010/10/25/afghanistan-cracks-down-on-internet-cafes-for-allowing-porn/.

15. "Porn Websites Among Most Visited in Islamic Countries," *Huffington Post*, November 14, 2012, accessed January 15, 2013, http://www.huffingtonpost.com/2012/11/14/porn-websites-among-most-viewed-islamic_n_2130317.html.

16. Kelli Morgan, "No. 1 Nation in Sexy Web Searches? Call it Pornistan," Fox News.com, July 13, 2010, accessed March 24, 2013, http://www.foxnews.com/world/2010/07/12/data-shows-pakistan-googling-pornographic-material/.

17. Eleanor Hall, "Professor Calls for a Global Anti-Porn Movement," ABC News, October 6, 2010, accessed January 15, 2013, http://www.abc.net.au/worldtoday/content/2010/s3030902.htm.

18. Ropelato.

19. Barna Group, "New Research Explores the Changing Shape of Temptation," January 4, 2013, accessed January 16, 2013, http://www.barna.org/culture-articles/597—new-years-resolutions-temptations-and-americas-favorite-sins.

20. "The Leadership Survey on Pastors and Internet Pornography," *Christianity Today* (Winter 2001), accessed January 16, 2013, http://www.christianitytoday.com/le/2001/winter/12.89.html.

21. "ChristiaNet Poll Finds that Evangelicals Are Addicted to Porn," Marketwire, August 7, 2006, accessed January 15, 2013, http://www.marketwire.com/press-release/christianet-poll-finds-that-evangelicals-are-addicted-to-porn-703951.htm.

22. Mike Genung, "How Many Porn Addicts are in Your Church," *Crosswalk*, June 17, 2005, accessed January 16, 2013, http://www.crosswalk.com/church/pastors-or-leadership/how-many-porn-addicts-are-in-your-church-1336107.html.

23. Barna Group, "Morality Continues to Decay," November 3, 2003, accessed January 16, 2013, http://www.barna.org/barna-update/article/5—barna-update/129—morality-continues-to-decay.

24. Jim Lo, "The Missionary and Porn," *Evangelical Missions Quarterly* (January 2003).

25. Ropelato.

Conclusion

1. Dan Pallotta, "Stop Thinking Outside of the Box," *Harvard Business Review Blog Network*, November 7, 2011, accessed January 18, 2013, http://blogs.hbr.org/pallotta/2011/11/stop-thinking-outside-the-box.html.

2. For more information on developing strategies in light of our global pressure points, see John Mark Terry and J. D. Payne, *Developing a Strategy for Missions: A Biblical, Historical, and Cultural Introduction* (Grand Rapids, MI: Baker Academic, 2013).

3. A variation of this diagram is found in my book *Discovering Church Planting: An Introduction to the Whats, Whys, and Hows of Global Church Planting* (Downers Grove, IL: InterVarsity, 2009), 412.

About the Author

J. D. Payne (PhD, Southern Baptist Theological Seminary) serves as the pastor of church multiplication with The Church at Brook Hills in Birmingham, Alabama. He has pastored churches in Kentucky and Indiana, and he served as a seminary professor for a decade. He is the author of several books on missions and evangelism. J. D. and his wife, Sarah, live in Birmingham with their three children, Hannah, Rachel, and Joel.

Endorsements

"Unreached People Groups"; "The West as a Mission Field"; "Globalization"—for all the world it sounds as though this book is just one more textbook for the classroom. Believe me, it isn't! It is for the classroom, of course. Missionaries and mission students will profit greatly by reading, studying and discussing these twelve "pressure points" in Christian missions today and tomorrow. But J. D. Payne has a way of taking topics off the classroom desk and putting them on the kitchen cupboard. And that's good—really good—because those of us who serve in the classroom and on the field desperately need the understanding, prayers, and support of those who "serve in the kitchen." World missions would benefit greatly if all mission-minded Christians would look into—and pray over—*Pressure Points*.

—DAVID J. HESSELGRAVE, PhD, PROFESSOR EMERITUS OF MISSION, TRINITY EVANGELICAL DIVINITY SCHOOL

In *Pressure Points*, J. D. Payne offers a compelling reflection on some of today's most pressing challenges to the advance of the gospel around the world. Understanding the issues with which missionaries on the ground are struggling, he helps lead the reader toward biblically-guided responses that advance Christ's Kingdom. I recommend *Pressure Points* to all those seeking to faithfully serve among the peoples of the world.

—M. DAVID SILLS, DMISS, PhD, ASSOCIATE DEAN OF CHRISTIAN MISSIONS, THE SOUTHERN BAPTIST THEOLOGICAL SEMINARY, AUTHOR OF *THE MISSIONARY CALL* AND *REACHING AND TEACHING*

Informative. Insightful. Inspiring. Convicting. Challenging. These are the words that come to mind as I reflect upon this important work by J. D. Payne. The world in which the church seeks to fulfill the Great Commission is changing more rapidly that we can adapt. The ability to think strategically and missiologically has never been more essential. *Pressure Points* will help us accomplish both of these necessary goals.

—DR. DANIEL L. AKIN, PRESIDENT, SOUTHEASTERN BAPTIST THEOLOGICAL SEMINARY

The twelve issues that J. D. Payne presents in *Pressure Points* serve as a wake-up call for the church. Ignoring these strategic trends could plunge Western Christianity into the abyss of irrelevancy. Recognizing and responding to these realities, however, will allow the message of Christ to resound gloriously throughout the nations.

—BILL JONES, PRESIDENT, COLUMBIA INTERNATIONAL UNIVERSITY

In *Pressure Points*, J. D. Payne has given us a rare combination of timely, well researched, readable, and practical content on some of the key issues facing the body of Christ. If we are to accelerate the fulfillment of the Great Commission in our generation, we cannot ignore these issues.

—STEVE MOORE, PRESIDENT, MISSIO NEXUS, AUTHOR OF *SEIZE THE VUJA DÉ: A FRESH LOOK AT CHALLENGES AND OPPORTUNITIES IN NORTH AMERICAN MISSIONS*

J. D. tackles issues of globalization and how it's impacting the church with the mind of an academic and the heart of an evangelist. This is a current, relevant, solid book that should be read and digested by anyone who is serious about reaching the world for Christ and understanding the challenges in front of us. Missiology and global studies are combined in this book not to give answers but raise the questions and clarify what engagement may or may not look like. If I were to recommend one missiology book today, this is it.

—BOB ROBERTS JR., SENIOR PASTOR, NORTHWOOD CHURCH, AUTHOR OF *BOLD AS LOVE*

Global Christians face constant pressures as we serve in the Kingdom, but we often fail to understand the sources of these pressures clearly. J. D. Payne's book powerfully illustrates some of today's most urgent pressure points and challenges us to act boldly as we respond biblically.

—JON HIRST, CEO OF GLOBAL MAPPING INTERNATIONAL, CO-EDITOR OF *INNOVATION IN MISSION*